# WHY GOOD GIRLS DON'T GET AHEAD...

### BUT

# GUTSY GIRLS

## <u>DO</u>

# WHY GOOD GIRLS DON'T GET AHEAD...

## BUT

# GUTSY GIRLS

# DO

*Nine Secrets Every
Career Woman Must Know*

## KATE WHITE

ARROW

Published by Arrow Books in 1996

3  5  7  9  10  8  6  4

Copyright © Kate White 1995

First published in the United Kingdom in 1995 by Century

Arrow Books Limited
Random House UK Ltd, 20 Vauxhall Bridge Road, London SW1V 2SA

Random House Australia (Pty) Limited
16 Dalmore Drive, Scoresby, Victoria 3179, Australia

Random House New Zealand Limited
18 Poland Road, Glenfield
Auckland 10, New Zealand

Random House South Africa (Pty) Limited
Endulini, 5a Jubilee Road, Parktown 2193, South Africa

Random House UK Limited Reg. No. 954009

A CIP catalogue record for this book
is available from the British Library

Papers used by Random House UK Limited
are natural, recyclable products made from wood grown in
sustainable forests. The manufacturing processes conform to
the environmental regulations of the country of origin

ISBN 0 09 939951 2

Printed and bound in Great Britain by
Cox & Wyman Ltd, Reading, Berkshire

To Brad.

# Acknowledgments

I'd like to thank all the gutsy girls who have inspired me throughout my life, including my mom, who always encouraged gutsiness (at thirteen she gave me *Bernice Bobs Her Hair* to read); my friend Andrea Kaplan, who said, "Why don't you turn it into a book?"; my fabulous gutsy agent, Sandy Dijkstra; and my wonderful, gutsy publisher, Maureen Egen.

# WHY GOOD GIRLS DON'T GET AHEAD...
## BUT
# GUTSY GIRLS
# <u>DO</u>

# CHAPTER ONE ......................................

# The Myth of the Good Girl

The day Julia Roberts's publicist telephoned my office and told me that Julia wondered what I had against her, I began to make an interesting discovery about myself—though I didn't realize it at the time.

First, let me give you the background on how Hollywood's hottest star had come to hold me in the same regard she had for the stripper Kiefer Sutherland was dating during their engagement. About a year before, as the editor-in-chief of *McCall's*, I'd commissioned an "unauthorized" cover story on Roberts, focusing on her mysterious hiatus from movies after she'd called off her wedding to Sutherland. It had sold like crazy on the newsstands. Now, the first rule of magazine newsstand sales is that if something works, you do it again— and that was my game plan exactly. The publicist had been furious about our first effort, and as soon as she got wind of the fact that we were planning yet *another* unauthorized cover story on her star client, she called me to protest. She said angrily that she'd always assumed that *McCall's* had high journalistic standards and wouldn't stoop to publishing a celebrity profile without interviewing the subject. She claimed that Julia had even asked her, "Does the editor of *McCall's* have something against me?"

Though most of our cover stories were interviews with celebrities, occasionally, when we were turned down by someone (as we had been by Roberts), we'd report the story using a variety of other sources. You'd be surprised at how many friends and relatives are willing to gab, though you also can discover that people have been warned to keep their mouths shut. In this particular case, the publicist was telling everyone, right down to the dolly grip operators on Julia's latest movie, not to talk to us, and so far this had resulted in a severe dearth of dirt. When I'd checked on the progress of the story one day, the researcher had looked up woefully from her desk and announced that the only new information she had was the fact that Roberts's nickname in high school supposedly had been "Hot Pants." Oh *great*, I thought. There was cover line potential (IS JULIA HAUNTED BY HER STEAMY PAST?), but the article would be one paragraph long.

Despite such roadblocks, I knew that eventually we'd end up with something. In the long run, this type of story often turns out to be the juiciest and most fun to work on because you've got to be more creative and resourceful.

Unfortunately Roberts and her publicist weren't seeing the fun in all of it. This was hardly the first time I'd had trouble with a cover subject. I once had to kill a cover story on a television star because the photographs came back making her look about as glamorous as a spokesperson for National Tartar Control Month. We heard from the star's publicist that she was very, very miffed. But this was the first time that I had been chewed out personally on the phone. Several days after the conversation with the publicist, I got a letter from her reiterating her annoyance. It was clear that Julia would certainly *never* agree to an interview with *McCall's*, and neither would any of the publicist's other clients. In fact, it almost sounded as if she was going to warn off all of Hollywood. Did this mean that I'd better get Marie Osmond and Pia Zadora on the phone fast because they'd be the only women I'd be able to recruit for a cover?

As I was packing up to leave the office that night, my assistant looked up at me and asked, "Does it bother you to get a letter like that? Aren't you worried that she might really *do* something?"

"No, it doesn't bother me," I laughed. And I meant it.

A few years before it *would* have bothered me. In fact, it might have even tortured me to know that someone was really mad over something I'd done and might say rotten things about me to other people. I liked being liked and hated not being liked—and I probably would have walked around for the next few days with a sense of dread, like the kind you experience when you are in the Federal Witness Protection Program. But those feelings just didn't happen anymore. Somewhere along the way I had stopped worrying about what people thought about me.

## MY MOMENT OF DISCOVERY

About a week later, a friend of mine in the company steamed into my office and handed me an article from the trade magazine *Executive Female* called "Why It Doesn't Pay to Be a Good Girl." The piece had been written by a woman who once had worked for me at another magazine and I assumed that was why my friend was showing it to me. As I glanced through it, however, I discovered, much to my amazement, that *I* was the focus of the story.

In the article the writer described herself as the quintessential good girl, someone who had always done what she was told, tried to make everyone like her, and taken on as much work as possible. She'd assumed that one day she'd be rewarded for such noble efforts. But much to her shock she'd seen many of the spoils she thought she deserved go to women like me. The author claimed I was the antithesis of a good girl, someone who broke the rules, didn't give a damn what people thought, made quick, bold decisions, and delegated all the grunt work to others (keeping control of the delicious, exciting stuff for myself). She said, with regret, that I had become her role model.

At first I thought, She's got it all wrong. I'd certainly heard psychologists talk about the concept of the good girl, the kind of woman who worries so much about pleasing other people that she neglects her own needs. Years before, I'd even written an article for *Mademoiselle* on the subject. If anyone had asked, however, I probably would have said automatically that I was a good girl myself.

But the more I considered it, the more I could see for certain that I was *not* a good girl. I was decisive, almost fearless, and I didn't spend time worrying about other people's opinions of me. That, after all, was why I hadn't agonized over the comments of Julia Roberts's publicist. I also realized that it was the reason for much of the professional success I'd had in the past few years.

Once, I *had* been a good girl. In fact, it's safe to say I'd been one for a huge chunk of my life. But over time—and especially during the past six years—I had changed rather drastically. What was I now? There seemed to be only one phrase for it:

I had become a gutsy girl.

## LET'S TALK ABOUT YOU FOR A MINUTE

If you bought this book, you probably responded on a gut level to the words *good girl* in the title. It's an expression that most women react to viscerally because we heard it over and over as we were growing up. Every time we jumped in a puddle with our party shoes on or cut off our doll's hair with nail scissors or blew bubbles into our milk or clobbered our little brother with his own weapon after he'd repeatedly tortured us, we were told, "Be a good girl," or "Good girls don't do that."

To be a good girl you had to follow the rules, act nice to everyone, and never talk back to your elders or superiors. Over time we learned to keep quiet and walk around the puddles.

Why did we acquiesce? Because throughout childhood and adolescence, not only were there reprimands for *failing* to be a good girl, there were also clear rewards for being one: we were applauded by parents and teachers and neighbors and just about everyone else, with the exception of guys in motorcycle jackets with tattoos that said *Born to Raise Hell*.

Now that you're out in the real world, good-girlism may appear to be working nicely, too. Bosses pat you on the back for a job well done and co-workers constantly say things like, "Thanks, you're a doll." But chances are you may already have begun to detect a fissure in the foundation of the good-girl way of life. You may, for instance, have come to feel the stress and strain that occurs from always trying to please, from constantly playing it safe, from being the one who never fails to get stuck with the dirty work. There is also a frustration from never confronting those who try to steal your thunder or your ideas. Think about it. Haven't there been evenings when you've left the office with your cheeks aching from keeping a frozen smile on your face all day?

I am here to tell you that the aching cheeks are the least of your problems. The real tragedy is that, despite the pats on the shoulder and the compliments, being a good girl actually undermines your career and prevents you from achieving maximum success. Sure, doing exactly as you're told, being nice and acting modestly worked at home and in school, but once you get out into the world of work, the dynamics change and you need to approach matters in a whole new way. The rewards go to women who make their own rules, take big chances, toot their own horns, and don't worry if everyone likes them.

This information may seem to fly in the face of reason. Right there in your office are probably loyal female managers who have done what they were told and have been promoted for doing so. But such "good" behavior will only get you so far. Studies show that managers tend to avoid risks, maintain momentum, focus on the short term, and work at balancing interests; *leaders,* on the other hand, take risks, stir things up, think long term, and pay attention to what *they* believe works best. To break out of the pack and become a real star in your company, you have to leave the Goody Two-Shoes behind— and become a gutsy girl. This approach is more essential today than ever. Currently, there's a glut of managers due to corporate downsizing and rightsizing. Though there are more routes to the top for women these days, the increased competition for these spots makes the proportion of opportunities smaller—and only the most dynamic employees will make the cut.

Was your last raise what you'd hoped for? Are you considered one of the dynamos in your department? Do you get the choice assignments? Does your boss's boss know who you are? Do you feel recognized for your contributions? Do you find your work pleasurable and exhilarating? If the answer to most of these questions is no, you may have worried at times that it reflects a lack of talent or skill on your part. But that may not be the case at all. You may simply be too good for your own good.

# "BUT DOES THIS MEAN I'M SUPPOSED TO BE BAD?"

Now, at this point you may be saying, "Whoa, wait a minute. Are you suggesting I start behaving like the Shannen Doherty of corporate America?" Not at all. A gutsy girl isn't a bad girl. She can be conscientious, hardworking, kind to her subordinates, and respectful of authority. But she also takes risks, charts her own course instead of doing exactly what she's told, asks for what she wants, gives the grunt work to someone else so she can focus on what's important (and fun), makes certain that the right people know of her accomplishments, and doesn't spend every moment trying to please people. Here's what a good girl and a gutsy girl look like side by side:

| A good girl... | A gutsy girl... |
| --- | --- |
| 1. follows the rules; | 1. breaks the rules—or makes her own; |
| 2. tries to do *everything*; | 2. has one clear goal for the future; |
| 3. works her tail off; | 3. does only what's essential; |
| 4. wants everybody to like her; | 4. doesn't worry whether people like her; |
| 5. keeps a low profile; | 5. walks and talks like a winner; |
| 6. waits patiently to get raises and promotions; | 6. asks for what she wants; |
| 7. avoids confrontations; | 7. faces trouble head-on; |
| 8. worries about other people's opinions; | 8. trusts her instincts; |
| 9. never takes risks. | 9. takes smart risks. |

When you bought this book, I don't think it was simply because the phrase *good girl* in the title hit home. I suspect it's also because the phrase *gutsy girl* captured your fancy. There's a part of you that's ready for change, that wants much more—and has begun to suspect you need a gutsier approach in order to get it.

But if you've been a good girl all your life, you're probably wondering how you can run against the grain of your nature.

I believe that even though you've followed the good-girl program growing up, it's not necessarily the response that's most natural for you. I believe that inside most good girls, there's still a spirited, adventurous, bubble-blowing, puddle-jumping, hair-scalping girl biding her time. When your face aches from smiling too much or your stomach hurts after a pathetic raise, it's just a signal of the tension from trying to keep her buried. Let me tell you a little bit about my own evolution.

# HOW I WENT TO BED A PUSHOVER AND WOKE UP A GUTSY GIRL

Sometimes I feel I was the original Goody Two-Shoes. As a fourteen-year-old, while many teenagers I knew were entering a defiant period, the only "wild" thing about me was that I set my hair with pink sponge rollers and Dippity-Do, and when combed out it looked like I had a woodchuck sitting on my head.

Oh, I longed to be wild, but I was afraid to break the rules. Here's a perfect example: My parents were fairly protective and they made my brothers and me wear boots in winter even if there were only two patches of snow on the sidewalk. Years later I mentioned to my brother Jim how embarrassed I'd felt trudging along in what seemed like forty pounds of rubber while everyone else had on Keds.

"Didn't it bother you?" I asked.

"Nah," he replied. "Mike and I always left our boots at Charlie Hagstrand's in the morning and picked them up on the way home."

It had never, not even once, occurred to me to break the rules that way.

My goody-two-boots tendencies continued all through school, as well as through the early years of my career. Sometimes I'd break out and do something surprisingly daring, and the result would be fabulous. But rather than think that gutsiness had worked in my favor, I'd feel as if I'd managed to get away with something and maybe I shouldn't try it again.

I started my career at *Glamour* magazine after winning their Top Ten College Women contest. After working at *Glamour* for six years as an editorial assistant and then a feature writer, I moved to *Family Weekly* (now *USA Today Weekend*), as senior editor and eventually executive editor. From there I went to *Mademoiselle*, where I was the executive editor in charge of the articles department. I was a hard worker, and though my boss considered me fairly spunky, I always minded my p's and q's. That approach, I assumed, was serving me well.

Then, just after I was promoted to the number-two position at *Mademoiselle*, I had a baby and everything began to change for me. I'd expected that in my case being a working mother would be fairly smooth sailing. My boss, an extremely smart and creative editor-in-chief, had a tendency to go hot and cold on employees, but I'd managed to remain in her good graces by following orders and agreeing with all of her insights. At times I felt like one of those dogs with the bobbing heads you see in the back windows of cars, but at least I felt safe in my job.

As soon as I returned from maternity leave, however, my boss turned icy toward me. After several years on the hot list, I suddenly had freezer burn. On my seventh day back, she called me into her office and said she was uncomfortable with the fact that I was now leaving at 5:00 P.M. every day and wanted me to stay until at least six in case any big ideas came up during that time period. She certainly had the right to say it, but to me it was a ludicrous request. We were, after all, a fashion and beauty magazine for twenty-four-year-olds. It wasn't as if someone was going to burst into my office at 5:45 screaming, "Stop the presses! Somebody just invented thong underwear!" Though I agreed to her demands, I left that night determined to get a job that would allow me to come and go as I pleased so I could spend enough time with my child. Four months later, after lots and lots of hustling, I was the editor-in-chief of *Child* magazine.

And that's when I started to scrutinize the way I approached my work and when I began, without even realizing it, to kick the good girl out of my system. You see, I really didn't have a choice. I wanted very much to succeed at *Child* but I also knew it would be tough to be effective in such a powerful position and also be a conscientious mother. I'd already discovered how crazy life was as a working mother. One night after I'd gotten home from *Mademoiselle*, I'd hurriedly dressed Hunter in his snowsuit so I could take him with me grocery shopping. As I pushed the stroller through my apartment building lobby, I noticed in the mirror that in my frantic state I'd put *his* little ski cap on *my* head. That moment seemed to symbolize the nuttiness of my life.

It was clear to me that in order to pull it off, I would have to change my work style. I was going to have to learn to make instant decisions, delegate like crazy, focus on the big picture rather than the details, and be adventurous in my thinking. And I was going to have to cease caring if people "liked" me.

So that's what I did. I took a gutsier approach to everything. And what's amazing is that as I experimented with this style, I discovered that it felt far more natural to me than the Little Miss Nice role I had played for so long.

A year and a half after going to *Child*, I was recruited to be the editor-in-chief of *Working Woman*. I was a little more than seven months' pregnant when I got the job; the owner said he chose me because of my gutsy new plan for the magazine. And a year and a half after that, I was recruited back to the New York Times Company to be editor-in-chief of *McCall's*. The good girl had bitten the dust.

After about four years at *McCall's* I was chosen last October to be the new editor-in-chief of *Redbook*, which had been brilliantly fashioned by Ellen Levine into a magazine for smart, sexy, gutsy women. I couldn't ask for more.

# THE TRIPLE BONUS OF BEING A GUTSY GIRL

Once I began to think about my transformation to gutsy girl and reflect on how it had affected my professional life—my whole life, for that matter—I decided I wanted to share what I have learned. This book is filled with strategies on how you too can become a gutsy girl. They come not only from me but from some of the very successful women I have met through my work.

A word of caution: Being gutsy is not without its consequences. It's not unlike putting on Rollerblades instead of walking shoes. You're going to get there faster, the ride will be exhilarating, and yet there's a chance of bruising your shins or even breaking your elbow. You'll find, however, that your new skills as a gutsy girl can help you deal with any flak that you get from taking chances.

You'll discover, as well, three amazing dividends from following the strategies in this book. The first I've already talked about: your career opportunities will open up dramatically as you begin to be bolder and stop trying to please everyone but yourself. Second, you will find yourself less a prisoner of your work as you learn to delegate, take shortcuts, and give yourself permission to relax. Being a gutsy girl actually has given me more personal time.

And finally you'll feel an amazing sense of relief as you let the gutsy girl out from her hiding place inside of you. It's wonderful to go home at night and not have to feel the ache in your cheeks from holding a frozen smile in place all day long.

# CHAPTER
# TWO............................................

# Are You Trapped in the Good-Girl Role?

I hope by now you're itching to read the strategies in this book and embark on a gutsier approach to your career. But before you do, it's important to do a little prep work.

First, you should spend time thinking about how your good-girl habits evolved. When you trace the pattern backward it's not only illuminating, but you're likely to end at a point in time when you were spunky, adventurous, and unafraid—and that can be very inspiring.

Next, you should figure out how the good girl in you operates. When is she most likely to take over? What effect has she had on your career up until now? Warning: It may be less obvious than you realize. Good-girlism, you see, is very sneaky, and wears a variety of surprising disguises.

## WHERE DO GOOD GIRLS COME FROM?

Good girls, I believe, are made, not born. In the past decade there's been a lot written about how women learn to put their own needs last and suppress their voices. Much of my understanding on this subject comes from conversations I've had with Ron Taffel, Ph.D., an extraordinary child psychologist and author of *Why Parents Disagree*, who writes "The Confident Parent" column for *McCall's*. Recruiting Dr. Taffel was one of the first steps I took after I got the job, because to me he had the freshest, most exciting views in the field of parenting. He works with individual kids and parents in therapy, and he also runs workshops for parents across the country.

According to Dr. Taffel, the seeds of the good girl are planted very early as a daughter observes the way the individuals in her home interact with each other and absorbs the messages her parents send.

While watching her mother day in and day out, she discovers the thousands of ways her mother takes care of everybody else. "A mother assumes primary responsibility for her family's needs," says Taffel. "When a father *does* participate, it's known as 'helping out.' "

The mother, even if she has a job, makes the arrangements for school, for play dates, meals, holidays, celebrations, dentist and doctor appointments, vacations, and trips to relatives. She buys the clothes, the underwear, the shoes, the toothbrushes, the birthday gifts (for her own kids as well as her kids' friends), the books, the Play-Doh and the paint sets. She drives for the car pool, makes the snacks, applies the Band-Aids, wipes the noses, cleans up the spills and messes, supervises the homework, calls the teacher, gets the camp applications, writes the thank-you notes. . . . It never stops.

A mother's responsibility includes not merely *doing* all these things, but constantly *thinking* about them, keeping a mental calendar and to-do list going day and night—what Taffel calls "The Endless List of Childrearing." This mental list is her province alone. It's safe to say that if she doesn't ever get

around to calling the orthodontist for a consultation, someone will have a lifelong overbite.

She is also what Taffel calls the family "gatekeeper," the possessor of critical information. If a child wants to know where to find a clean pair of socks or a library book he was reading, there is only one parent who knows for sure.

The message a daughter hears through all this is that one of the most important jobs a female has is considering and taking care of others' needs, and in the process that often involves putting her own needs aside.

That's not all that's going on. In her home, Dr. Taffel explains, a daughter is also encouraged to be "the best little girl in the world." When she takes a toy from another child, talks back to her parents, refuses to follow an order, she is told, "That's not nice," or "Be nice," or "Be a good girl." Because her not-so-pleasing, aggressive side is so often admonished, she may become ashamed of it—and eventually repress it.

"Anger is the signal that it's time to be assertive," says Dr. Taffel, "but if you are told repeatedly that it's wrong to be angry and you don't let yourself feel anger, you lose the signal that you need to let your assertiveness take over."

Boys, too, are admonished for their bad behavior, but it's often done with a wink or what Taffel calls a "double look." It's as if the parent is saying, "You shouldn't have done that—but I'm proud of you because you did. It means you're not a wimp or a sissy."

Now, certainly this was the way it used to happen, but haven't things changed? Aren't we giving girls a whole new set of messages?

Marsha Gathron, associate professor of health and sports sciences at Ohio University, who has studied self-esteem in young girls, says that she feels the problem has gotten even worse. "Young girls are being hit just as hard today if not harder than several generations ago," she says. "Many of the

same variables are still there that make girls doubt themselves. Plus we no longer have the strong family ties that might help some girls get beyond the messages."

Dr. Taffel believes that though we've made progress in raising kids without the strong sexual stereotyping of the past, the good-girl message still comes through loud and clear, not only at home, but through television, advertising, books, and other conduits of society's attitude. Sometimes it's done with such subtlety that we don't even notice.

Consider the latest edition of the classic board game Chutes and Ladders, billed as "an exciting up and down game for little people." In the game, players (kids ages four to seven) move along a playing board, sometimes landing on ladders that allow them to take shortcuts, and sometimes landing on chutes that force them backwards. The ladder squares depict kids being rewarded for good behavior and the chute squares show them facing consequences for bad behavior.

Here's where it gets interesting. There are twelve boys on the board, compared to seven girls. In the examples in which the boys get to move up the ladders, they are being rewarded for a *variety* of good behavior, including some heroic stuff: returning a lost purse, saving a kitty. The girls are all rewarded for housework: sweeping a floor, baking a cake. As for bad behavior, there are twice as many high jinks for the boys. The girls' naughty behavior, what little there is of it, includes eating too much candy and carrying too many dishes. The boys' is all action oriented: riding a bike without holding on, breaking a window playing ball, and walking in a puddle. Twenty million sets of Chutes and Ladders have been sold since its creation.

Even when we attempt to be fair, we blunder. Take a look at the hugely successful book series for young kids, the Berenstain Bears. The books are charming, informative, and full of politically correct references to nurturing dads and working

moms. But here's what Sister Bear and Brother Bear fantasize about in *Trouble with Pets*, published in 1990, when they're anticipating getting their first dog.

> Sister thought about dressing it in doll's clothes and pushing it in her doll carriage. She thought about introducing it to her stuffed toys. Perhaps they could have a tea party. . . . Brother's thoughts were quite different; he thought about winning the blue ribbon at the Bear Country Dog Show. He thought how fine it would be to shout "Mush!" as his great dog pulled him through the deep snow.

In other words, Sister wants to sit around looking pretty and acting pleasant. Brother wants to be a leader and a winner.

## THE GOOD GIRL GOES TO SCHOOL

Any good-girl message that comes through at home soon gets reinforced at school. Some research over the past two decades has revealed that there is extraordinary gender bias in schools, and that it continues in strong force today. Social scientists Myra Sadker, Ed.D., and David Sadker, Ed.D., authors of *Failing at Fairness: How America's Schools Cheat Girls*, who have conducted twenty years of research, say that girls are systematically denied opportunities in areas where boys are encouraged to excel, often by well-meaning teachers who are unaware of what they're doing. Male students, the Sadkers report, control classroom conversation. They ask and answer more questions. They receive more praise for the intellectual quality of their ideas. Girls, on the other hand, are taught to speak quietly, to defer to boys, to avoid math and science, and to value neatness over innovation, appearance over intelligence. In one school contest the Sadkers observed, the "Brilliant Boys" competed against the "Good Girls."

In the early grades, girls routinely outperform boys on achievement tests, but that's only one part of "schooling." "There's the *official* curriculum, which calls for doing well on tests and homework and getting good grades," says David Sadker, "but then there's also the *hidden* one. This curriculum involves speaking up in class, raising questions, offering insights. It helps a student develop a public voice. Girls aren't encouraged to develop this public voice. They are rewarded for being nice and being quiet. Their high grades lull them into a false sense of security that they are doing what they must to be a success. It's only later that they pay a price for having been encouraged to be a spectator, to not speak up."

By the time girls graduate from high school, they lag, as a group, far behind their male counterparts.

Year after year of these messages, both in school and on the home front, can become internalized. The most widely known research on what happens to school-age girls is by Carol Gilligan, professor in the Human Development and Pyschology Program at the graduate school of Education, Harvard University. In studies Gilligan found that there is a "silencing" of girls that occurs as they move from the elementary grades into junior high. Up until that point, she says, they seem filled with self-confidence and courage, and they're candid about what they feel and think and know. But as they enter midadolescence and become aware of society's expectations of them, they start to get more tentative and conflicted. The conventions of femininity require them to be what Gilligan calls "the always nice and kind perfect girl."

Thus, Gilligan says, girls experience a debilitating tension between caring for themselves and caring for others, between their understanding of the world and their awareness that it is not appropriate to speak or act on this understanding. They are uncomfortable about how people will feel if they get mad or aren't "nice." The girl who is insistent on speaking and desires knowledge goes "underground," says Gilligan, or is overwhelmed.

When girls look to grown women for inspiration, they may not get any help. Gilligan says that women, in the name of being good women, model for girls the "repudiation" of the playful, irreverent, outspoken girl.

Though some experts have criticized Gilligan's theories, I think many of us can't help but see ourselves when we read her words. You're automatically transported back into sixth or seventh grade, feeling the fatigue of always trying to please and the stress that results from constant vigilance over your own words and behavior. By the age of eleven or twelve you probably discovered the importance of being "liked," and what that required. Popular boys are often boisterous and mischievous, but popular girls are generally careful about their words and their behavior. As soon as this sank in, you locked that smile into place and tried not to sound opinionated. You worried about what you were going to say before you said it, while you were saying it, and after you said it.

And come to think of it, you weren't really supposed to be saying much at all. You were told it was important to let boys do the talking and so you listened, smiled, listened. You learned quickly that no one likes a girl who hogs the limelight. And God forbid you ever did anything unconventional that would draw attention to yourself and make some loud bully of a boy suddenly take particular notice of you in class and decide that you were the one who would be crucified for your clothes or your complexion or your breasts.

I can remember extraordinarily well a moment when I began to shut down part of myself in order to be liked. During my early grade-school years, I had this devilish streak in me, even though I was also pretty shy. In sixth grade this cute and cocky boy named Kevin transferred to our school and into my class. Everyone, boys and girls alike, fawned over him, and as the year went along he got kind of big for his britches. Where I grew up, in upper New York State, the first of May was celebrated by kids exchanging May Day baskets they made by pasting crepe paper on old oatmeal and saltine cracker boxes and filling them with candy. This particular May Day I decided I wanted to get Kevin's attention, but instead of fawning, I tried a more irreverent approach that I thought he'd appreciate as a cocky kid. I made the rattiest looking May Day basket with water-stained, ripped crepe paper, then filled it with stones, and left it on his desk just as everyone was coming in from lunch.

Well, you would have thought I'd yelled the words *sexual intercourse* at the top of my lungs. A hush fell over the class as kids realized what had happened, and once it was discovered I was the culprit, they looked at me in horror. I tried to make light of the situation, but that night I went home feeling something I had never experienced in school before: shame.

From that day forward I did my best to hold that little devil down. I got with the good-girl program that is reinforced all through adolescence. Abigail Cook, a friend of mine who is a trader on Wall Street, puts it this way: "If I could have hung a motto over my bed in high school it would have been: 'Be nice, you'll be liked, you'll get married.' "

Though many of Gilligan's theories were developed over fifteen years ago, educators and researchers say they see the same dynamics at work today.

Barbara Berg, dean of the upper school of Horace Mann, a private school in New York, and author of *Crisis of the Working Mother*, says that she witnesses many young girls caught in the good-girl trap and unable to feel a personal sense of empowerment. "A girl who was being verbally harassed by some boys came to my office lately for help," says Berg, "I suggested that one step would be for her to tell the boys that she didn't want them to do that. She said that she couldn't. She was worried that if she did, they wouldn't like her."

In school, a girl may find herself in a constant and draining state of *either/or*. You can be pretty *or* powerful, you can be popular *or* smart.

So take a trip back to your early life and think about when and how the good girl in you began to emerge. You may remember how wonderful it felt before you had to put on the muzzle.

# THE GOOD GIRL GOES TO COLLEGE

For some girls, college is the time to try to break out of the good-girl mold. And yet by then the message is pretty ingrained in many of us and there may be a reluctance to challenge the "system," or at the very least an inability in knowing how to begin. Dr. Gathron says that as part of her research on women and self-esteem, she asks freshmen women to tell her what they think and feel about themselves, using adjectives and descriptors. The results are the same from year to year. "What is so amazing is that they sit and *ponder*," she says. "They have a hard time coming up with anything. As women, we're told all our lives how to act and what's expected of us. We haven't thought enough about ourselves and what we feel and think."

As a member of the first coed graduating class of Union College, I found myself the first year in a class with twenty men and only one other woman, and through the entire semester the professor never once made eye contact with either of us. On Halloween we wore matching pumpkin outfits with green hoods over our faces, just to see if we could get a rise out of him, but even that didn't do the trick.

# THE GOOD GIRL GETS A JOB

By the time you enter the work force, you've had over twenty years of good-girl training—and you really know your stuff. With so much reinforcement, it makes perfect sense that you would follow the good-girl principles in your job—and at first glance, it actually seems to work. Because they may have a vested interest in keeping you in your place, some bosses and most of your co-workers will praise you for your good behavior. You'll be complimented for following the rules, being patient, doing the lion's share of work, and not taking any stupid risks. I just loved the line that the *New York Times* wrote in a short bio of Justice Ruth Ginsburg after the approval of her nomination to the Supreme Court: "She handled her intelligence gracefully—sharing her schoolwork, avoiding the first-person singular and talking often of having been in the right place at the right time." It was as if the *Times* was saying, "*See?* It pays to be a good girl. Women should put everybody else ahead of themselves and attribute all of their success to luck."

But despite what the "evidence" appears to indicate, the kind of good-girl behavior that won you praise at home and A's in school ultimately won't advance your career. Why not? Because the standards have changed.

"There are no daily quizzes in the world of work," say the Sadkers. "This is where boys learn the value of having developed that public voice, the one girls are discouraged from using in school."

Career success isn't about learning the textbook answers to questions and repeating them back on a test. It's about generating fresh, creative ideas that make people go "Wow." It's not about waiting to be called on. It's about asking for what you want. It's not about making everyone like you. It's about getting things done effectively even if you have to ruffle some feathers—or kick some butt.

That's not to say that being a good girl will prevent you from earning *any* points in your job. As a good girl you might make a reliable manager—because you take care of your charges, follow rules, and work your tail off. But that's never going to make you a star.

Okay, sometimes the gods smile down on good girls and reward them for their hard work. But for the most part, good-girl traits will sabotage your chances for gaining a key leadership position.

Robin Dee Post is a clinical psychologist in Denver who has worked with many career women in therapy and believes there are two distinct ways women sometimes sabotage their success, and also create unnecessary stress for themselves.

The first involves relationships at work—how we respond to bosses, co-workers, and subordinates.

"Because we've been trained to be nice and always think of others, it makes it harder for us to put our own needs first in the work place," Post says. "As a result we have trouble confronting others when we have a problem with them. This same factor also makes us reluctant to let others know of our accomplishments."

The second way involves putting excessive demands on ourselves—due perhaps to excessively high demands or criticism when we were growing up. That, Post believes, leads to perfectionism, procrastination, and an overcommitment to work.

# HOW MUCH OF A GOOD GIRL ARE YOU?

By now you may feel that you already have an idea of your own specific good-girl patterns, but trust me, it's trickier than you might expect. Sometimes, when you *think* you're performing at your best, the good girl in you is actually busy undermining your efforts. Here's a lesson from my own life.

It happened the summer I was thirty-one, working as the articles editor at *Family Weekly* magazine, which was a Sunday newspaper supplement similar to *Parade* and was later purchased by *USA Today*. My job appeared to be pretty stable, until, that is, the day the editor-in-chief unexpectedly resigned to become editor of *GQ* magazine. I'd just put the finishing touches on plans for a three-week adventure cruise around northern Greenland and the news made me feel as if I had just been rammed by an iceberg. Would he take me with him? I wondered. If not, how would things change for me at the magazine? Was my job in jeopardy? Two days after my boss's announcement, I was called into the publisher's office and informed, much to my surprise, that I would be in charge of running the magazine while a search was conducted for a new editor-in-chief. And here was the icing on the cake: my name was being added to the list of candidates for this job.

As I left the publisher's office, there was one immediate thought flashing through my mind: Well, I guess I'm not going to get to see any puffins or polar bears this year. But once the news sank in, I was exhilarated, and I felt a burning passion to put my stamp on the magazine during my stint as acting editor. I also realized that I really, *really* wanted the job. The publisher had told me that like all the other candidates, I had to submit a long-term proposal for the magazine to the top people in the company. I vowed that when the big guys were done reading mine they'd have to collect their socks from across the room.

Over the next weeks—and what turned out to be months—I threw myself into the job, doing everything possible to make the magazine snazzy and get it to the plant on time each week. The publisher had asked that I send him memos on upcoming cover stories, but other than that he left me to my own devices. I didn't make any attempt to contact him, figuring it was best to leave well enough alone. My proposal for the magazine was completed in two weeks and I sent it by interoffice mail to top management, keeping my fingers crossed.

There were a few hairy moments, mainly with the staff: morale got very low because it was taking management so long to make a decision, but I was as pleasant as could be, bending over backwards to get people to like me. My biggest headache was with the senior editor, who called me into her office one day, told me to shut the door, and announced that she had the publisher wrapped around her finger and could make or break my chances for the job. I suggested we have dinner and talk over the situation.

Finally, after three long months, the publisher phoned and asked me to join him the next day for lunch at the Palm, a famous New York steak house favored by middle-aged salesmen with arteries as hard as curtain rods. I knew I was about to learn my fate, and something told me that the news wasn't good: the job was probably going to someone else and I was about to get surf-and-turf as a consolation prize.

Twenty minutes after we sat down, the publisher still hadn't mentioned my job, though he'd twice called me "Princess," which I took as a sign that a power position probably wasn't in my immediate future. The biggest omen occurred when I returned from the ladies' room. Not wanting to seem like a sissy, I'd asked him to order me a glass of red wine while I was gone. "Bad news," he announced as I sat down again. "They won't bring your wine until they see a picture ID."

Over coffee I learned that indeed I wasn't going to be editor-in-chief. The guy they'd hired was about twelve years older than I, with "lots of experience." They gave me a title change and a raise and I got some consolation from the fact that my proposal was supposedly the best of the lot. What I told myself through my disappointment was that I'd lost out because I was too young. I believed that my day would come and that years later I would look back and realize that everything had worked out for the best.

It's only now, over ten years later, while writing this book, that the truth has finally hit me: I failed to get the job of editor-in-chief not because I was too young at the time but *because I'd been a good girl*. I'd retreated into the woodwork, rationalizing that a low profile would help my case. I'd tried so hard to make the staff like me that they viewed me as desperate and thus, powerless. And I'd never taken any steps to demonstrate to top management that I had a burning passion for the position.

What I should have done during my months as acting editor was work closely with the publisher and allow him to see what a capable editor I was. I should have been more of a boss to the staff, showing them that I wouldn't tolerate insubordination or whining. And I should have asked top management for the opportunity to present my proposal in person and then convince them that I was the one for the job.

Sure, things ultimately worked out very well for me, but who knows what opportunities might have unfolded if I'd gotten the top job at such a young age.

Recognizing how much I acted like a good girl during that time has been a turning point for me. It's allowed me to see that good-girl behavior often masquerades as something we consider to be positive. You tell yourself, for instance, that you're cautious or modest or patient, and you assume that's the mark of a real pro. Yes, sometimes caution and modesty and patience have their place. But left unchecked, they are career quicksand.

So when you're considering how much of a good girl you may be, look below the surface. If you're not certain how ingrained your good-girlism is, the quiz below will give you some clues.

# THE OFFICIAL GOOD-GIRL QUIZ

1) Your boss calls a meeting and announces to you and the rest of the staff that he wants each of you to come up with suggestions for a presentation geared to winning new clients. He offers several guidelines, based on what's worked for clients in the past. You
   a. put together a thoughtful, well-written plan, following his instructions to the T.
   b. come up with a plan that's outside the parameters your boss suggests—in fact, it's partially inspired by something you saw on MTV—but you sense it could work beautifully, so you submit it anyway.

2) You've recently been put in charge of a new area in your company and you've spent several weeks researching and developing a set of goals for the area. Two of your new employees want you to add several of their pet interests to your list. You
   a. hear them out but decide not to incorporate their ideas into your overall plan because they don't fit with your mission.
   b. include their goals because you know it's important to make them feel part of the team.

**3)** Your boss asks you to provide her with written suggestions on how to improve some of the services your company provides. She says she wants it in two weeks. When the date arrives, you

    a. give yourself a few extra days to polish your report, counting on the fact that your boss will appreciate your efforts.

    b. hand in the report, knowing that though it's good, you would have loved to have had another week.

**4)** Your secretary arrives late for the fifth time in two weeks. She has mentioned to you that she is having problems with both her boyfriend and her sinuses. You

    a. call her into your office and explain that you want her at her desk promptly at nine each morning.

    b. say nothing, because she's basically responsible and you can count on her to sort things out. Scolding her will only make things worse.

**5)** At a meeting of your department, you bring up an idea you've been cogitating on for a few weeks. Your boss seems mildly curious and she throws it out for discussion. A few colleagues mumble polite encouragement, but one co-worker, someone you consider a real pal, announces that she doesn't feel the idea has much merit. She backs up her opinion with several statistics. You feel

    a. embarrassed and hurt.

    b. curious about how she knows so much on that particular subject.

**6)** One of your clients sends you a terrific note praising your performance. You

    a. Pass along the letter to your boss with a note that says, *FYI.*

b. Tuck it in a file you keep of letters and notes like this, just in case you might want to use it in the future.

7) In the past year you've taken on more and more of your boss's responsibility, allowing him to assume more exciting projects himself. Your boss has consistently praised your performance and announced the other day that if it weren't for the budget freeze, he'd promote you. You
   a. trust your boss to come through when he has the money.
   b. make an appointment to see your boss and say that you'd like him to consider giving you a new title, with a raise to follow when he has the money.

8) You hear through the office grapevine that a colleague has called an important resource of yours, ostensibly just to check out a lead. You
   a. step into your colleague's office and say that you expect him to check with you before he contacts a source that you have cultivated.
   b. bide your time, deciding that you *will* challenge him, but when you have actual evidence that he's been poaching on your territory.

9) On two separate occasions you find several of the people who work for you whispering behind partially closed doors. After asking yourself if something could be up, you
   a. tell yourself you're being paranoid.
   b. tell yourself something is definitely brewing and try to find out what it is.

10) You accept a new job that you sound perfectly suited for. Three weeks after starting, however, you realize that you've got far more to learn than you realized. As you lie in bed at night you think

a. I can do this, I can do this.
b. Oh, no. I'm in over my head.

## SCORING YOURSELF

Give yourself 1 point for every *b* answer to questions 1, 3, 5, 7, and 9, and none for *a* answers to those questions. Give yourself one point for every *a* answer for questions 2, 4, 6, 8, and 10, and none for *b* answers to those questions.

If you scored 9 or 10 points, you're gutsy as hell, and I'm tempted to say give this book to a more needy friend. But since the title of the book intrigued you, there's a chance a good girl is lurking inside, and you may need reinforcement on your gutsiness (or some of your answers may have reflected how you would *like* to behave rather than how you generally do).

If you scored between 5 and 8, you've already developed some gutsy instincts, but you've got much more to learn.

If you scored under 5, your good-girlism is pretty seriously ingrained. You need help, but trust me, there's hope.

## NO, YOU ABSOLUTELY DO NOT HAVE TO ACT LIKE A MAN

As I've talked about some of the ways gutsy girls do business, you may have begun to wonder whether acting gutsy really comes down to acting like a man.

That, after all, was the advice offered to women when they first poured into the workforce in the seventies. You may have read or at least heard of the mega best-selling book *Games Mother Never Taught You* by Betty Harragan. It burst on the

nia, who treats many women with classic good-girl tendencies, says she's found that they start out feeling very reluctant to try something new or adventurous because they worry that there will be dire consequences. "But when they do finally make a move, they discover that instead of something bad happening, it is often something very good," she said. "And that realization is totally liberating."

The fact is that unlike at home and in school, your gutsy efforts will sooner or later be rewarded.

A friend of mine, Mary Jo Sherman, who is president of Levit and Sherman advertising agency, puts it this way: "When you're growing up and you don't act like a good girl, your mother sends you to your room. But at work, being gutsier wins you a major client or some other kind of prize. As you see what it nets you, you become braver and braver."

Let's start with the very first strategy of a gutsy girl.

# CHAPTER
## THREE ....................................

# Strategy #1: A Gutsy Girl Breaks the Rules

When I set out to write this book, I spent a lot of time thinking back on the best lessons I'd learned during my career. Initially, everything I considered automatically came from the years after I graduated from college and went into magazine publishing. And yet one day I realized that I'd gotten one of the most enlightening lessons the summer I was seventeen and employed as a fountain girl at Howard Johnson's on Route 9 in upstate New York.

I was a terrible waitress, with timing so bad that I served people their soup with their main course and their bill as they were pulling out of the parking lot. I'd go home at night feeling exhausted and drained, stung by the insults hurled in my direction ("She must be *new*" was a frequent one). Even the cook seemed to dislike me. At HoJo's you had to use certain abbreviations when you put an order through, such as OR for an order of two eggs. A few days after I started, someone asked for eggs sunny-side up, and I improvised by writing on the dupe sheet: *OR SSU*. No sooner had I put it through when I heard the cook bellow from the sizzling kitchen, "What the hell do you think this is—the navy?"

There was only one consolation: as a Howard Johnson employee, I was allowed to eat all the ice cream I wanted—though much to my chagrin, not with any of the toppings available to customers, like hot fudge or Reddi Wip. It was absolutely taboo for a waitress to help herself to the extras.

Three weeks into my summer there, a girl named Tracey joined the fountain-girl contingent and things started to improve for me. She was spunky and fun, completely unfazed by people who barked complaints about the one-quarter-inch-thick steaks or shouted for extra packets of wet wipes. During slow times she talked about the wild guys she dated or her favorite hobby, racing her parents' car down back country roads. When she worked the night shift and didn't feel like waiting on people, she would stick up a sign, visible only to people coming in the front door, that said COUNTER CLOSED.

One day our lunch breaks coincided, and as we headed downstairs to the employee lounge together, walking by the manager who always checked out the employee lunch selections, I mentioned how bummed out I felt having to eat my ice cream without any toppings. Tracey gave me a devious laugh. "Oh, we can fix that," she said. As soon as we were alone in the basement, she dug her spoon deep into her ice cream, revealing an amazing cross section. At the bottom of the bowl was a layer of nuts and cherries, topped by whipped cream, then hot fudge and finally the ice cream.

"It's an upside-down sundae," she announced with a smirk.

I was stunned by both her nerve and her ingeniousness. From then on I ate an upside-down sundae every day for lunch, and going into work stopped being so onerous.

Only now, however, have I come to see that there are much broader applications to what Tracey showed me. Here's the real lesson: If you want to eat the cherry in life, to say nothing of the hot fudge and whipped cream, you've got to break the rules.

And that's the very first strategy of a gutsy girl. If you hope to be a star in your company and a standout in your field, you must, at times, make your own set of rules for what you're doing. You must listen to what they tell you to do and then you must twist it, toss it, or turn it upside down so that the result is brilliantly bold and different.

In many ways it's the foundation of every strategy in this book because in each case you're going against the grain of what you've always been told to do. You shouldn't, of course, just break the rules helter-skelter. Your rule breaking should be in the context of your overall mission (see Chapter 4), but the reason I'm going to talk about rule breaking first is that it will loosen you up to think about the most imaginative mission for yourself and your department.

## THE RULES OF RULE BREAKING

The idea of breaking rules makes you nervous, doesn't it? After all, you've always been told that those who follow the rules are rewarded and those who break them are punished—sometimes very, very badly.

This is a "truth" that some experts say is reinforced for girls far more than for boys. Dr. Allana Elovson, a developmental and social psychologist in Santa Monica who is an expert on gender bias and has done workshops with many parents, says that the messages boys and girls get about rule breaking are very different. "The unspoken message is that 'Boys will be boys,' " she explains. "It's okay for them to be bad. On the other hand, we expect little girls to be more civilized. If they break the rules, we come down much more heavily on them."

In their research on sexism in schools, Myra and David

Sadker found that girls are often rewarded for passivity whereas boys receive encouragement for challenging the status quo. For example, in instance after instance they saw teachers stress to students that they needed to raise their hands before responding to a question. When the discussion became fast-paced, the rule was often swept away. Boys, the researchers found, called out eight times more often than girls. Whether boys' comments were insightful or irrelevant, teachers responded to them. However, when girls called out, there was a fascinating occurrence. "Suddenly," say the Sadkers, "the teacher remembers the rule about raising your hand before you talk. And then the girl, who is usually not as assertive as the male students, is deftly and swiftly put back in her place."

The women who get ahead are those who learn to ignore the warnings they've been given about breaking the rules. If you look at the work history of a gutsy girl, you see that she has made her mark by ignoring "orders" and taking some bold, innovative step that wowed her bosses and left her peers grumbling in exasperation, "I can't believe they let her get away with that" or "I would have done that but I didn't think you were supposed to."

If you're going to be a gutsy girl, it's time to think about creating your own upside-down sundae.

One of the gutsiest rule benders I know is Nancy Glass, the anchor of one of the top-rated syndicated TV news magazine shows, *American Journal,* and a former senior correspondent for *Inside Edition*. Over the years, she's landed exclusive interviews with a rogues' gallery of contemporary antiheroes that includes Jeffrey Dahmer, Amy Fisher, Imelda Marcos, and Roseanne's parents. Nancy has always told me that in her career she lives by the principle, *There are no rules*.

"People love to tell you the rules," she says. "When I first started as a reporter, I was always told that to set up an interview with someone, you had to go through the standard channels, like the person's publicist or lawyer. But that's often a dead end because they really don't want the person to be interviewed. They'll just tell you, 'No, Mr. So-and-So isn't available for interviews.' So over time I found the one way to guarantee getting an interview was to just show up unannounced on the person's lawn. You can't imagine their shock when they first see you, but after a few minutes, after they've gotten to talk to you, they begin to trust you and feel receptive to the idea of being interviewed. I've come to believe that every opportunity is a vacuum waiting for you to fill it with your *own* rules."

# NO, I'M NOT SUGGESTING YOU NEED TO LIE, CHEAT, OR STEAL

It may sound as if I'm suggesting you land a chopper on someone's lawn. Not at all. In fact, it's probably best to leave that to renegade TV reporters with big blond hair. Nor am I suggesting that you lie on your resumé, cheat on your expense account, ignore company guidelines, or call your boss a butthead.

To understand what I mean by rule breaking and why it's an essential strategy, you have to consider where rules comes from—and their fallibility. Many rules are in existence because they once worked quite nicely, but there's every chance that they have become meaningless over time. People follow them out of habit, because "that's the way we've always done things here." Other rules or directions have been set up by well-meaning people who unfortunately lack skill, talent, or creativity. These rules are supposed to offer guidance, but they only serve to hinder you.

Often, the only way to get substantial results and break out of the pack is to bend one of these rules or ignore it completely. Won't this get you into trouble? It *might*. But it's best to worry about that later. U.S. Senator Barbara Mikulski, a human dynamo who got her start as an activist by preventing the construction of a sixteen-lane highway through her town, told me that the motto that sums up so much of what she's done is, *It's always better to ask for forgiveness than permission*. And trust me, if they like what they see, you won't be on your knees.

The first chance I had to discover the benefit of a little rule bending was when I entered *Glamour* magazine's Top Ten College Women Contest as a college senior. My school had chosen me to be their candidate and I wanted more than anything to win—partly because the prize was a ten-day trip to Great Britain, but also because I saw it as a way to break into the magazine business. The application called for a photo, a description of your campus activities and awards, and an essay on the goals you had for the future. I spent two days trying to figure out what kind of essay would help me stand out from the pack of wildly popular, rich, and beautiful girls from colleges like Wellesley and Smith. Finally I decided that I would break the rules of the contest and write an essay on why, at twenty-two, I had no goals. I stated that in the chaotic seventies it seemed inappropriate to have some definitive road map for the future. Six months later I was having tea and scones at the Churchill Hotel in London.

Unfortunately, like many good girls, instead of recognizing how much the rule breaking had paid off for me, I assumed that I'd managed to get away with something. It took many years for me to see that all my big successes had resulted from *not* doing what I was told.

There are several variations on rule breaking and at a given time one will work better for you than another.

# #1: DO SOMETHING THAT NO ONE HAS THOUGHT OF OR DARED TO DO BEFORE

Perhaps the gutsiest form of rule breaking is to go out there and do something that's never been done before, even something that's considered taboo for your field. That's what Andrea Robinson, president of department-store marketing at Revlon, did when she took over Ultima II several years ago and launched a makeup line called "The Nakeds." It was makeup that had only a hint of color and made you look like you weren't actually *wearing* any. Robinson was one of the first women we profiled after I took over *Working Woman* and I've always admired the sheer, so to speak, gutsiness of what she did. Until then makeup had always been about color, of course, and more than a few people told her that The Nakeds were bound to fail.

But Robinson felt women were ready for something quite new. "I saw a different attitude taking hold in the nineties," she recalls. "We had just come out of a decade where everyone was very coiffed and manicured and luxuried to death. I thought women didn't want to look like they spent all that time on themselves anymore. The philosophy behind The Nakeds was, *Look like yourself, only better.*"

The Nakeds was a major hit. The company even had to run ads apologizing to customers for not being able to get the product to them as fast as they wanted it.

# #2: DO WHAT YOU'RE SUPPOSED TO DO—BUT IN A TOTALLY DIFFERENT WAY

In certain situations what's called for isn't something spanking new, but rather a bold variation on what you've been doing all along.

After Cheryl Deaton became principal of West Forest Elementary school in Opelika, Alabama, a school at which the majority of students were poor, she soon came to realize that the standard approach to running a school and helping kids learn just wasn't working there. Test scores were the lowest in the district and many students eventually dropped out of school. Gradually, Deaton and the team of people she worked with began altering the way they imparted knowledge and managed students.

"We got rid of textbooks in certain classes, like English, and replaced them with contemporary books that we knew kids would be attracted to," says Deaton. "Textbooks have a canned representation of things. In libraries kids don't take out books that are old. They read what's attractive and fun and has a nice front cover. In the age of Nintendo, kids want things with sex appeal, for lack of a better word."

Though Deaton's step of "throwing out the books" generated lots of press, her innovative strategies went far beyond that. The curriculum was changed to offer more music and art classes than schools traditionally offer, in order to have an "easy way for kids to communicate and be successful." She even changed the way kids were disciplined in school. "Instead of punishing kids in the punitive, pruned-up mouth way that schools are known for, we began helping a child model appropriate behavior."

Today, test scores have improved dramatically and the school has won major awards, including the $750,000 Next

Century Schools Award. Deaton is now chief officer for Educational Improvement for Montgomery Public Schools.

# #3: DO SOMETHING THAT DOESN'T APPEAR ANYWHERE IN YOUR JOB DESCRIPTION

And sometimes rule breaking is a matter of rule *extending* or *expanding*, going outside the parameters of your job description to make the kind of impact you can't make *within* those parameters.

Now, your first reaction might be, "Hey, I don't want to overstep my bounds." But today that's become a necessity. There was a time when getting promoted was a result of doing a fabulous job within the framework you'd been given. But those were in fatter years. Now, you must do that just to *keep* your job. To move up, you have to take on some of your boss's responsibilities or contribute something of value that may not have been requested of you but is nonetheless viewed as beneficial to the company.

When Claire Brinker was working as the ad director for Red Cross Shoes, a division of U.S. Shoe, her job responsibilities were to create ads and sales promotion events for Red Cross Shoes and two other subsidiaries. Unfortunately, Red Cross was a declining business, due in part to the association people had with the name. Brinker felt it was essential that the company find ways to grow the business, which had a target audience of women age thirty-five and above.

One of the observations she'd made was that women everywhere seemed to be walking. She could also see that women who walked faced a paucity of shoes to choose from. "If they went into an athletic footwear store," says Brinker, "they'd end up with some teenager asking, 'How fast do you run?' The more I read about the popularity of walking, the more I realized that our company should develop a walking shoe. And we should sell it not in athletic footwear stores but in department stores, where women over thirty-five were more comfortable shopping."

So Brinker went to management and pitched the idea, even though that wasn't one of the things she was "supposed" to do under her job description. It took lots of effort ("My persistence could have been compared to Chinese water torture"), but she eventually sold them on the idea—and the result was the Easy Spirit Walking Shoe, the third-ranked brand of walking shoes in the country.

Today Brinker is director of corporate marketing at U.S. Shoe. She also played a major role in the success of the Easy Spirit dress pump—which was marketed brilliantly by showing women wearing the pump as they played a fast game of basketball.

I know that even as I champion the benefits of breaking the rules, you probably still consider it a scary proposition. But here's what I've learned. The first time you break the rules, it's not nearly as frightening as you think it will be; in fact, it can be downright exhilarating. It has always reminded me of the thrill I felt the first time my mother let me strip to my underpants and run through the sprinkler in our backyard.

# WARNING: DO NOT CONFUSE GUSTO WITH GUTSINESS

If you're smart and a hard worker, someone whom other people think of as a go-getter, you may be telling yourself right now that you are already a rule breaker. But go-getting is not the same as rule breaking. I've seen good girls on my staff congratulate themselves for being whirlwinds around the office, but when the dust has settled, all they've done is follow orders and take care of the basics.

## TEST YOUR RECORD

To find out how much of a rule breaker you are, ask yourself these questions:

In the past month have you

- done something in your job that's never been tried before?
- used a fresh new approach to get a task or project accomplished?
- solved a nagging problem that no one has ever bothered to tackle?
- taken on a major responsibility that wasn't in your job description?
- presented an idea to your boss that made her say, "Wow"?
- done something that made half your peers green with envy?

If you answered NO to most of these questions (or "No, but . . ."), it's time to strip down to your metaphoric underpants and jump through the water.

## DO NOT PROCEED UNTIL YOU CONSIDER THESE TWO POINTS

Okay, before you do start jumping in, it's important to realize that only a certain kind of rule breaking will pay off for you. It must directly or indirectly

1. make money for your company, OR
2. save money for your company.

Now, that seems pretty obvious, but good girls have a tendency to gravitate toward earnest projects that sound noble on paper and involve lots of scurrying around, but ultimately don't help the bottom line.

At one of the fashion magazines I worked at, an editor on my level in another department told me one day in a self-congratulatory tone that she had just gotten permission from the editor-in-chief to develop a stringer system for the magazine. Young women from around the country would be paid a small retainer to keep the magazine posted on trends and stories in their area. There would be stringers in Minneapolis and Miami, Tucson and L.A. Here a stringer, there a stringer, everywhere a stringer stringer. The editor said this had never been done at the magazine before and she was thrilled to have gotten it off the ground. As I offered her a strained, "That's great," all I could wonder was whether I should have thought of the idea myself.

But you know what? Readers of the magazine wanted to know what the hottest styles were and the tell-tale signs of guys who would never commit, not what people were doing in Des Moines. The stringer system might have charted new territory but it did nothing for the business. It fizzled just a short time later.

# SIX EASY WAYS TO COME UP WITH A WOW IDEA

Okay, you're ready and eager to make a gutsy move, to break, bend, or extend the rules. But where do you begin? How do you find the ingredients for your own upside-down sundae?

One of the points that struck me as I pored through management books in my job as editor-in-chief of *Working Woman* was how little information exists on how actually to generate a bold, creative idea or strategy. These books are filled with information on how to do the maintenance part of your job effectively: supervising people, handling your boss, managing your time, but little on going beyond the basics. You're not likely to find a chapter called "How to Knock Their Socks Off."

In part that's because we assume you can't teach people how to conceive bold, gutsy ideas—they're supposedly second nature to certain individuals. But I think there are several strategies that you can train yourself to use effectively.

# 1. Fantasize About What Turns You On

Some of the gutsiest moves involve paying attention to your *own* needs as a human being, as a consumer, even if it means ignoring the common wisdom in your company about what people want. You know what you like, what you buy, what you rely on, what you really get the hots for. That's incredibly valuable information. My assistant, Amy, once told me that her favorite magazine covers were those that looked so delicious that she felt a strange urge to lick them. I realized that that was one of the best guidelines I'd ever heard, far better than any I'd gotten analyzing lots of numbers.

Unfortunately we tend to leave our secret or crazy yearnings behind when we walk into our jobs. We're encouraged to focus on lots of numbers and adhere to principles developed by people who haven't been away from their desks in decades. If you pay attention to what gets your juices flowing, you are likely to hit on an approach that may seem renegade, but in the long run it could turn everything around for you.

This is how I got one of my biggest career breaks in my twenties.

At the time I was a junior writer at *Glamour*, in charge of turning out short little pieces for a section called "The How to Do Anything Better Guide." It was a good starter job in the articles department, but I knew there was no way I could stand out if I was forever relegated to subjects like "How to Make a Bathing Suit from Two Bandanna Scarves." I would have to write a major feature in order to establish myself as an important player.

Most of the articles in *Glamour* at the time were reporting pieces, like "Dating and Mating: How Much Have the Rules Changed?" But I just couldn't get interested in doing a piece that focused on trends or provided lots of helpful tips. What really fascinated me most were some of the issues I was facing in my own life as a single woman living in a shabby apartment building in New York City, and I wanted to write a sad and funny first-person article about my experiences. The magazine rarely ran essays, but I felt that if my heart was aching as a single girl, so were others'. Over the next two months I wrote a story about being single, about being terrified of living alone, about having a lackluster social life and a telephone that rang so infrequently that it seemed as vestigial as my appendix.

The moment after I put it on the editor-in-chief's desk, I began to panic. They never did pieces like the one I'd just handed in and I worried that she'd see me as a real kook. (I imagined her calling Personnel and saying, "Help, there's a girl on my staff who thinks there are giant seed pods under her bed.") But as it turned out she loved the article and crashed it into the next issue. I got dozens of letters from readers who said things like, "How did you know how I feel? I could have written those words myself." And I was asked by the managing editor to begin churning out essays on any subject that I felt passionate about.

Looking at her own needs was exactly what Andrea Robinson did. Despite the preponderance of colors at makeup counters everywhere, she herself wanted makeup that would enhance her appearance without making her look like she was wearing much. "I couldn't find the kind of makeup *I* wanted," she says. "I wanted to look like I was wearing *something*, but I didn't want to seem painted with a lot of blue, pink, or red."

## 2. Ask Yourself, "What Are They Really Looking For?"

I've been talking about how you need to step outside the boundaries you've been given, but how do you do that without going in the wrong direction and getting lost—or arrested for trespassing? One trick is to consider the ultimate goal of the project you're working on, regardless of whatever guidelines or instructions you've been given.

Recently I talked to this charming, high-powered young woman, Amanda Schatz, associate manager of 3 Arts Entertainment, who had worked in an entry-level position at the L.A.-based Creative Artists Agency. One day her boss and she were discussing how the agency might become more of a force in the New York market, and he suggested she make a list of people they could develop as contacts. As she thought about the assignment later, she decided to do something far more expansive. He had given her a "starter project," but the ultimate goal, she knew, was to establish a plan for New York. She wrote a four-page memo on how to get into the New York market and her boss was so blown away, he sent it around the company. A few days later, Mike Ovitz, the president and one of the most powerful people in Hollywood, called to tell her how impressed he was.

# 3. Live By the Phrase, "What More Could I Do?"

No matter what description you've been given for either an assignment or your overall job, you have to always be wondering how to make it broader, bolder, more exciting.

The woman who has taught me the most about ignoring the parameters—or to use the vogue expression of the day, "pushing the envelope"—is Andrea Kaplan, the vice president in charge of corporate communications for Gruner & Jahr. You give her parameters and she starts toying with them, like a cat with yarn, and it's such a kick to watch. She got her start in public relations working for a small, prestigious firm that represented a variety of clients. She'd only been working there for a few months when she began to go outside the lines and expand the responsibilities she'd been given.

The client she'd been assigned to was a fashion magazine, and she'd been told by her boss to write four or five press releases each month, based on material from each issue, and pitch them to the Associated Press and other wire services. The hope was to get at least one story on the wires for every issue. Each month the drill was pretty much the same—her boss never suggested she waver from the basic plan.

In March, as Oscar night approached, Kaplan suddenly saw an opportunity to do something special. The magazine had an entertainment editor who was charismatic and photogenic, and Kaplan thought it would be great fun to turn her into a commentator on Oscar night fashions—Who was wearing the most outrageous outfit? Who was in the most danger of falling out of her dress?—for one of the New York stations. At first people on the magazine reacted by saying, "But there's nothing in the magazine about Oscar dressing." Kaplan's response: "So what? The TV stations don't care." One station eagerly jumped at the opportunity, the entertainment editor was a smash, and the magazine was delighted. From then on, press releases became just a part of what Kaplan did each month.

If I were to call up Kaplan and say, "I just sold a book on how women can learn to take a gutsier approach to their jobs," she'd say, "Fabulous! Why don't you do one of those day-at-a-glance calendars with a gutsy goal on every page? And why don't you sell the rights to the movies? It can be the sequel to *Working Girl*."

# 4. Imagine the Wackiest Solution Possible

Sometimes you need to step outside the lines, and sometimes you need to go even further, to contemplate something outrageous, perhaps even downright naughty. At *McCall's* I got to know and learn from one of the columnists, Alexandra Stoddard, the renowned decorator and author. Stoddard is very sophisticated looking but she's got an adventurous, irreverent side as well. She told me once that when she was first working as a decorator, she landed two young, blue-blooded clients who had inherited a spectacular home. They wanted her to make it beautiful, but there was a very big hitch: they hadn't inherited any *cash*. Stoddard would have to operate on an itsy-bitsy budget. That, however, didn't mean she could zip over to Sears. This was a couple who loved elegance and wouldn't be satisfied with anything "cheap."

After several days of cogitating, Stoddard came up with a plan that would solve her problem. It was daring, even sort of zany, but she thought the couple would go for it. She went to Knoll Associates and bought woven-leather porch furniture for their living room. Though it was top of the line for a porch, it was far less expensive than living room stuff. It was also chic and beautiful and sensuous, and their friends would think they were marvelously avant-garde using it in their living room. An extra dividend: They could move it to their porch once they could afford real living room furniture.

# 5. Look at a Problem While Standing on Your Head

One of the rule-breaking strategies I use most frequently is to look at a situation from a different vantage point than the one that I or everybody else has been using. This works especially well with nagging problems, those that have been dogging your department forever but no one ever gets around to solving. (Hint: The nice thing about solving a nagging problem is that it seems less renegade to nervous superiors than other forms of rule breaking.)

When I joined *Family Weekly* as articles editor, the nagging problem was that we could only pay $500 tops for an article. At the time most magazines paid up to several thousand dollars for a piece, so we were forced to use young, inexperienced hack writers. This didn't stop the editor-in-chief from trying. He was a terrific journalist who was constantly making statements like, "Let's see if Nora Ephron will write it," and you'd walk out of his office muttering, "Yeah, fat chance. She gets five hundred dollars to cover her lunch expenses on an assignment." I once did call Nora Ephron about doing a piece for us and she said no with the same disdain she would have used if I'd asked her if she'd be interested in buying a device to remove toe beards. Despite the abuse we took from these hot writers, we continued to call them because we wanted to add class to the magazine.

The obvious solution was to pay more, but the company had no intention of coughing up the money. One day I started looking at the problem from a different direction. Instead of focusing on all the good writers who had turned us down and wondering whether there would have been any way to convince them, I started thinking about the few big names who had said *yes*. Was there a common denominator? In most cases the reason they'd consented was that they liked the idea of mass exposure—we had 28 million readers—during a time they were promoting a book they'd written. What, I wondered, if instead of going after big-name writers randomly, we went after only the ones who had books out, or better yet, books just coming out? And instead of approaching them directly, we'd go through the publishing-house publicity departments, which would be our ally in making the appeal. Over the next year or two I landed James Michener, Gail Sheehy, Betty Friedan, Alvin Toffler, Margaret Truman, and Robert Jastrow, among others, to write cover stories, all to coincide with the publication of their new books.

# 6. Steal a Great Idea from Someone Else

I don't mean to just out-and-out steal it, but rather figure out if there's some derivation that can work for you. Too often when we see a fabulous idea we get so busy kicking ourselves for not being the one to think of it that we neglect to consider how we can apply the principles to our own projects. One of my most successful column ideas was an indirect steal from someone else.

When I was at *Working Woman* I was always trying to find

ways to include more real working women in the magazine, but profiles of them never rated very well. Readers were most interested in profiles of the glamour pusses of industries or in straightforward management and career-strategy pieces. One day I was at a magazine awards ceremony and one of the columns that was being honored was "All I Know" from *Golf* magazine, a feature in which a famous golf pro talked about how he had mastered a particular golf dilemma, like sand traps. Walking out of the luncheon, I came up with a column called "How I Did It." Each month a different working woman would talk about a specific accomplishment: selling an idea to top management or adding new life to a tired product. It was an instant hit in the ratings. Though straight profiles of ordinary women weren't appealing, readers were obviously interested in the strategies they had used to get results.

One of my favorite steal stories comes from Wendy Kopp, president and founder of Teach for America. I met her after we had selected her for a special feature in *McCall's*, and she's by far one of the most dynamic young women I've ever met.

While Kopp was at Princeton in the late eighties, she worked on several extracurricular projects that made her aware of the problems many public schools across the country had attracting high-caliber teachers. She eventually decided to develop a teacher corps, composed of recent college graduates, that would go into poor areas to work. But how could she possibly recruit graduates for such an unglamorous post? This, after all, was the eighties. All around her at Princeton, Kopp watched as her classmates were being lured by investment banking firms: These firms offered prestige and security, they recruited aggressively, and they paid major bucks.

What Kopp finally decided to do was steal their techniques. She couldn't deliver money, but she could offer the other three benefits. "To guarantee prestige, we only accept the top candidates," says Kopp. "The program is a two-year one so there's a sense of security, of being rooted for a while. And we recruit really aggressively on campuses."

# HOW TO BREAK THE RULES AND NOT GET BURNED

But if you start playing loose with the rules, isn't there a chance you'll get into trouble? Nancy Austin, the dynamic management consultant and author whom I hired as a columnist for *Working Woman*, told me recently that whenever she holds seminars with people about work, Anita Roddick's name frequently comes up. People are dazzled by her, the quintessential rule breaker who created the environmentally correct and very successful cosmetics company The Body Shop, and they talk about how much they'd love to be her. And yet when Austin suddenly asks, "Would you hire her?" there's always a deafening silence as people realize that no, of course not. They wouldn't want a wild card like that working for them.

Fortunately the atmosphere in many companies today is changing to accommodate those who have the guts to venture into exciting new territory. Also, rule breaking, done right, doesn't have to threaten your superiors. If you do something smart and effective that's not part of the official "plan," your boss is not likely to punish you if it makes her look good.

Men have an intuitive sense of this because their rule breaking so often got a wink as they were growing up. A CEO, who asked to remain anonymous, recently described the difference between how men and women often handle the assignments he gives them. "The women will do exactly as I ask, working hard but never going outside of the outlines I give. The results are thorough and professional—but unexciting. The guys, on the other hand, veer off from the outline and come up with something really innovative that grabs me by the seat of my pants."

That said, you can run into trouble as a rule breaker. There are several ways you must protect yourself:

1. Establish a track record of competence. You'll be much more likely to get maverick ideas accepted if you've already proven you can handle the basics of your job.

2. Get the support of your boss—and anyone else necessary. There are two basic reasons why you need your boss's blessing if you are going to do any rule breaking. Even if you have a good relationship, surprising him with anything out of the ordinary could make him think you're headstrong or too big for your britches. If you *don't* get along, rule breaking will come across to him as close to mutinous.

   But that's not the only reason you must have his support. It paves the way for cooperation on the part of others you'll have to deal with. My friend Stephanie Cook, senior VP at Bloom FCA advertising agency, calls this "borrowing the power."

   Before Cheryl Deaton used any of her throw-out-the-books strategies as principle, she got the support of her bosses—the kids' parents. She also brought local businesses into the loop, generating their support and cooperation because they could help fund many of the projects.

3. Know the landscape. Senator Mikulski gave me the following advice: "You can't push the envelope until you know how the post office works." Even if you've been empowered by your boss, the climate has to be right for

gutsiness. Step back, observe, note what happens to those who make bold moves. Are they rewarded? Are they considered dangerous or bitchy or too out on a limb?

4. If someone tells you, "That's not the way we do things around here," repackage your idea to seem less threatening. Or offer to try something both ways—the standard and the more experimental.

5. Share the glory. Lyle Sussman, a professor of management at the University of Louisville who wrote a management-strategy box each month while I was at *Working Woman*, once told me that "stars today must be team players." It's just a fact of life that many of your peers and even some of your subordinates are not going to be overly pleased to see you stepping boldly into the limelight. They may feel jealous, threatened, overwhelmed with a sense that you are on a very fast train and they are being left behind at a dusty little small-town station. They may allow their negative feelings simply to simmer or they may go so far as to act on them, sabotaging what you're doing, criticizing you behind your back. However, if you demonstrate that you are taking them on the train with you by including them in your projects, you have a chance that they will support your efforts rather than hurt them. Frankie Sue del Pappa, the attorney general of Nevada, says her motto is "Put your arms around as many people as possible." When she has a news conference, she includes everybody she can up there with her.

# THEY SHOOT MAVERICKS, DON'T THEY?

What if you do all you're supposed to do to protect yourself and they still try to pounce on you?

You have to be prepared for the fact that it *could* happen. Grace Joely Beatty, senior partner of the management consulting firm Gardner-Beatty in Rancho La Costa, California, says that despite the fact that there are many open-minded companies today, there are still plenty of good-old-boy operations that are immovable. You bring up one creative idea after another and they are shot down like clay pigeons. It just might not be worth your while to stay.

"Many companies want 'maintenance managers' who don't innovate," says Beatty. "If you're the creative entrepreneur type, you won't do well there. IBM is such a company—look where it is now. Women, especially, think they can change such a climate through sheer willpower, but actually the *smart* move is to just get out and go to a more dynamic environment."

If you stay and try to play by the rules, you'll be miserable. If you buck the system, they'll do their best to *make* you miserable.

Use your rule breaking strategies to find your way out. Recently I had the chance to talk to Jeannie Boylan, the police sketch artist who helped solve the Polly Klaas abduction and murder. Unlike the majority of police sketch artists, who have witnesses pick out features from books, Boylan simply has witnesses describe suspects from memory—after she allows them lots of time to relax and feel comfortable. Though her sketches have consistently proven to be uncannily like the actual criminals, the police departments she worked in often made her life hell because she didn't do things the standard way. After many years of trying fruitlessly to work within the system, she told me that she's found career happiness working as a freelance consultant to law enforcement agencies.

# GO FOR THE GUTSY MOMENT

There's one last thing I want to say about rule breaking, and it relates not to projects or assignments you're working on but to personal behavior. I feel I should begin with a warning similar to one of those you see on late night TV commercials that goes something like, "Do Not Attempt This in Your Own Home." What I'm about to say is fairly provocative and risky advice and yet, it seems to have worked for many gutsy girls. When you need to get their attention, try something brash. You take what could be an ordinary moment and turn it into a gutsy one.

This story might help explain what I mean.

When I was in ninth grade, the nun who taught the honors English class always gave us the most remarkable assignments, like writing essays on current affairs and composing our own ballads. One week our project was to write and give a presentation on something the other kids in the class knew nothing about. I decided to make my presentation on rats—don't ask me why—and I prepared a grisly talk on thirteen things about rats you'd never heard. My favorite was the fact that if left alone in your basement, two rats could turn into a million in just a three-year period.

I knew my talk would have the kids squirming and I decided to give it a twist. Using an old fur coat from the attic and a piece of electric wire, I fashioned a life-size rat, which I hid in a paper bag behind the podium. During my talk I could tell I had the class spellbound—a few students even looked nauseous. When I finished with my nasty rat facts, I told the class that I thought it would help if they had a first-hand look at what I'd been talking about. Then I pulled the fake rat out of the bag. Boys shrieked, girls squealed, and at least half the class dived under their desks. And the nun? She sat there grinning from ear to ear.

That was the first time I saw the impact of delivering the unexpected.

One of my oldest friends is Merrie Spaeth, who runs Spaeth Communications, Inc., in Dallas and was formerly President Reagan's media adviser. She believes that rule breaking shouldn't be limited to how you handle the responsibilities of your job. Her philosophy: "I think there are some situations that call for doing something gutsy with your personal behavior."

It's hard to give any specific advice here. You just have to let yourself get a feel for certain situations and decide if a gutsy, unexpected move on your part could prove to be an advantage. A friend of mine says that a turning point in her career occurred the day she had to give a speech about her area to a group of top managers whom she had never dealt with before. A few minutes before going on she decided not to stand behind the podium but to take the mike and deliver her presentation from the middle of the floor. Not hiding behind the podium forced everyone's attention on her and infused her presentation with energy and spontaneity. From that day forward, she said, she was on the fast track in the eyes of management.

Earlier in Merrie Spaeth's career, a colleague arranged for her to meet the late William Paley, founder and retired CEO of CBS, who was looking for someone to write his speeches. She was warned, however. Paley could be difficult and stubborn, and he had already gone through a bunch of male speechwriters, even though they had been deferential and eager to please. And by the way, she was told, you never called him anything but Mr. Paley.

Merrie listened and realized that if she was going to win him over, she would have to seem in command, unlike the yes-men. When she walked through the door to meet Paley for the first time, she stuck out her hand and said, "Hi, Bill, I'm Merrie Spaeth." He chuckled and it was the beginning of a great relationship.

# FOUR .....................................

# Strategy #2: A Gutsy Girl Has One Clear Goal for the Future

A couple of weeks after I signed the contract to write this book, there was a brief moment when I wondered if the publisher was going to call me and say that they still loved the *idea* for the book, but would I mind if Janet Reno actually wrote it. She'd just taken the heat for the FBI's Waco, Texas, fiasco, even though she wasn't really to blame. It was a refreshingly different tactic for a politician and the media loved it. A newspaper ran her picture with just the word GUTS over it. Janet Reno seemed to be the epitome of the gutsy girl.

A year later, however, the media wasn't being so flattering. In fact, the *New York Times* published a story with *this* headline: DRIFT AND TURMOIL IN JUSTICE DEPT: AURA OF CONFUSION LINKED TO ATTORNEY GENERAL'S PERFORMANCE.

Here's a highlight from the article:

> These officials say the Attorney General has seemed indecisive, losing focus by taking on too many issues, hopscotching from project to project. . . . The officials, including some who say they hope she succeeds, insist

the public impression of Ms. Reno as the gutsy Florida prosecutor who took responsibility for the tear gas assault in April is at odds with the Attorney General they see every day.

What had gone wrong? How had the original gutsy girl ended up in such a big fat mess?

It's quite simple. No matter how gutsy Reno was about tackling individual situations, she had failed to come up with a strong, succinct vision for her "company"—or if she had, she hadn't articulated it clearly to those who worked for her. With a vision in place at the Justice Department, it would have been possible for Reno to pick projects without the appearance of hopscotching around—because any project that didn't fit the plan wouldn't be awarded priority. And it would have been easier to stick to decisions if there was a well-defined mission.

The moral of this story is that it's not enough to have a gutsy personality, to be someone who can take risks, create her own rules, and accept responsibility for any mistakes her staff makes with firearms. You have to have a vision, which becomes the *context* for any kind of gutsy moves you make or rule breaking you do.

Several years ago, R. N. Kanungo and Jay A. Conger, professor and assistant professor respectively of organizational behavior at Faculty of Management, McGill University, in Canada, took a look at leadership within organizations in order to strip the aura of mysticism from it. They found several behavioral components of charismatic leaders that distinguished them from noncharismatic ones. The charismatic leaders, they concluded, tend to "possess a sense of strategic *vision,* or . . . some idealized goal which the executive wants the organization to achieve in the future." In other words: A gutsy girl must have a gutsy goal.

# WHY GOOD GIRLS DON'T FOCUS

Focusing on one clear goal or mission is hard for a good girl. She's been programmed to "do it all," to try to please everybody, and so she's reluctant to limit the dimensions of her vision. If she sacrifices certain projects or products, she worries that she won't be viewed as the wonder girl who can handle ten things at a time. Or she believes that she'll be letting down people whose needs don't get included in the plan.

Fear can also keep a good girl from developing a big plan for the future. Recently a friend complained to me about a good girl on her staff who had failed to form a vision for her area. "At first I thought she was overworked, that she didn't have time, so I gave her an extra two staff members," she said. "When that didn't work, I thought it was my fault—that I'd led her to believe that all the big-picture stuff had to come from me. So I told her she had complete freedom to chart the course for her area. And she still didn't do it. I've finally come to believe that the idea of creating a mission scared her. She'd be accountable for it. A lot less risky approach was to force me to take that responsibility."

I feel that's been true for some of the good girls who've worked for me. If you've got your head lowered and your nose close to the grindstone, where you focus on the minutiae of every day, there's less chance you'll be hit by one of the SCUDs whizzing by. It feels safer that way.

And yet that's an illusion. Without a goal, you won't know where you're going. The people who work for you will feel adrift, confused, and quite possibly angry (and though they aren't likely to run squealing to the *New York Times*, they might do equally mutinous things). Your boss will sense that while you may be putting in the hours, you don't have much to show for it.

# WHY YOU NEED A BIG VISION EVEN IF YOU HAVE A LITTLE JOB

Now, if you're fairly low on the company totem pole, you may be thinking that this chapter isn't for you. A vision is something for someone who oversees an entire operation, or at the very least, a department. But no matter how small your domain— even if you are only in charge of managing *yourself*—you need a vision, a goal for your area and an awareness of how the steps you take can make that goal achievable. Your vision, of course, must directly relate to the overall vision of your company.

When I was in my twenties, I was stupidly reluctant to do this because I thought a vision was something my bosses were supposed to come up with, whereas I was supposed to follow their lead.

Looking back, however, I realize how much more effective I would have been in my job if I'd created a "big picture" in my mind, plus how much more focused I would have appeared to my bosses.

Of course, creating a vision is best done when you arrive in a new job. If you've been in your job and don't yet have one, you need to get your head out of the file drawer and start looking toward the sky.

# HOW TO CREATE YOUR VISION

Words like *vision* and *mission* have a tendency to sound very grand and idealistic, like something starring Glenn Close on the *Hallmark Hall of Fame*. Yet a good mission should be grounded by reality, even while it's smart and innovative. Ian Wilson, a senior management consultant at SRI International, says that a vision is a "coherent and powerful statement of what the business can and should be. . . ." *Can* and *should* are the key words. The word *can* has to do with your resources and capabilities. A vision is meaningless if it calls for funding or skills or peoplepower your department doesn't possess or can't *ever* possess. The word *should* relates to the values and aspirations of management.

When you create your vision, it should be as specific as possible. Name your destination and also spell out the directions for getting there. And the more criteria you can offer for measuring success the better.

How do you figure out what the destination should be?

Probably the smartest thing I've learned about visions is that you should always begin by looking at what you've got. What's been the plan for your area or department up until now, the goals everybody has been asked to work toward? Within that framework, what's good, what's bad, and what's turned seriously ugly? That sounds like a pretty basic approach and yet it's amazing how often in business people choose not to follow it. They come in with a kind of snooty attitude and develop a plan based purely on how things "ought" to be or how they were done at the last place they worked. They ignore the strengths or even trample on them. They either fail to deal with the weaknesses or end up perpetuating them.

In the magazine industry there have been editors-in-chief who take over an existing magazine with a vision that sounds dazzling when described in the trade publications or the *New York Times* media column but shows no respect for what was working about the magazine to begin with. The new editor will then use the letter-from-the-editor page to explain how weak the previous magazine was. The reader is left thinking he or she must have been a real doofus to have been reading it.

# FIND THE STRENGTHS—NO MATTER WHERE THEY'RE BURIED

If you've inherited a real dud of an area, there may not be many strengths to speak of. But chances are there's something worthwhile to examine—it just may be buried under layers of dust or discontent.

I had the opportunity to talk not long ago to Dr. Clyda Rent, the extraordinary president of Mississippi University for Women, a school she has totally revitalized and put on the map in five years. Though the college had lost the reputation of its golden years, when she was being recruited for the job she could see, just walking around the campus, that there were fabulous assets. The campus was absolutely gorgeous, with twenty-four historic landmark buildings. There was an excellent faculty. Dr. Rent eventually learned that there were also many distinguished alumnae, including Pulitzer Prize–winning author Eudora Welty. One other major plus: The school was very affordable.

Over time, however, people had lost sight of these strengths. "Everyone was so beaten up by politics of closure threats that they didn't see what a fabulous jewel they were sitting on," Rent says. The buildings, for instance, had become run down. There was no mention in any of the campus promotion pieces of the great alumnae.

Rent's vision began to emerge, and it was all about using the strengths she saw, rather than creating something brand-new. She decided to refurbish the buildings and promote the alumnae and publicize the affordable cost even more. She would build MUW's reputation as a school with a beautiful setting, terrific faculty, a distinguished history, and low tuition. During the past five years "the W" has grown at a rate that is twenty-five times the average of the other Mississippi universities and four times the national average. The National Wingspread Conference named MUW one of the "Twenty Model Colleges" in America for "exemplary undergraduate education."

In probing for the strengths, you have to be open to any source that can offer clues. That means the people you work with, including subordinates, and those on the outside, too. There's a legendary editor-in-chief in women's magazine publishing who recently took over a new magazine. Every person I know who went to interview for a position there told me that she asked them, "What would you do if you were me?" How shrewd she was. She pumped everybody, gathering, for free, people's ideas and insights.

And remember that the strengths you develop should be those that will work in the marketplace in the future as well as today. "The strengths I saw at MUW were ones that I thought would serve students well in the twenty-first century," says Dr. Rent.

# THE AMAZING BENEFIT OF REALLY BAD NEWS

It's one thing to probe for the good. Probing for the bad can be tougher, especially if you're just now creating a vision for a job you've had for a while. Good girls don't like discovering that everything isn't perfect, because they take bad news personally. One of the observations I've made about gutsy women I know is how unintimidated they are about disastrous facts. They don't try to rationalize them or scoot them under the rug.

And that's because hiding in the midst of bad news are often the seeds for a brilliant plan. The Kanungo and Conger study found that charismatic executives, unlike noncharismatic ones, "recognize deficiencies in the present system, actively searching out existing or potential shortcomings in the status quo." From there they determine how weaknesses can be transformed into opportunities.

When Laurie Ward, president of the interior design company Use-What-You-Have Interiors, started her very successful business, it was based completely on what she saw as the weaknesses in her old business.

She'd been a classic interior designer who went into people's homes and did a total overhaul. But there were several aspects of the job that began to bother her. "As a traditional decorator, you make your money on a percentage of everything the clients buy," says Ward. "It's in your interest, therefore, to get them to purchase as much as possible. But I didn't like telling a client to start over when they had a really good foundation. I'd often realize that a certain piece of furniture that didn't seem to work in one room would actually look terrific in another, and I'd almost have to tie my hands together not to move it."

So Ward chucked the old way of doing things and started a business that calls for clients to pay her a flat fee for an overall consultation about their home. She makes suggestions about what purchases they might make but also encourages people to keep any furniture and accessories that actually *work*.

In my early weeks at *Child* magazine, when I was trying to develop my goals for the magazine, I got handed two pieces of really bad news that made me feel like sitting at my desk with my head in my hands, muttering "*oy vey*" for an hour or two. But both of these killer facts ended up helping me find my way.

Up until my arrival, the one-year-old *Child* had been positioned as a parenting magazine for very, very upscale mothers and fathers, featuring articles on how to find a camp with a good reputation, plan a perfect birthday party, teach "good table manners," and enable your child to achieve his career goals. There was nothing on the down-and-dirty basics of parenting, like what to do when your kid screams that you're a poo-poohead in front of a restaurant full of people or insists you lie on the floor outside his door until he falls asleep at night. That type of advice was usually left to *Parents* magazine, a publication geared more for middle-class mothers, to dispense.

Was this a good vision for *Child*? It was almost impossible to tell. The magazine certainly looked beautiful and vibrant, but there was no data yet available on readers or how they responded to the magazine.

The first piece of bad news I got was a demographic study on parents that had been initiated before I arrived. According to the study, if you counted up the number of parents who made over $75,000 a year and had kids under five, parents for whom *Child* was marketed, the total was about 126 in the entire United States. Great, I thought, no audience. The study also showed, however, that once you looked at families with income around $50,000, suddenly the audience got much bigger.

The other piece of bad news was the results of a questionnaire I crashed into the issue that was closing when I arrived. I'd asked readers to rate each article in the issue. All of these articles had been assigned before I got there, with the exception of a little sidebar I added to a piece on birth order called "How to Make Each Child Feel Special."

Well, unfortunately, many of the more highbrow pieces didn't score very well. The highest-rated piece in the entire issue was actually the little box on making each child feel special. But what that revealed was actually pretty fascinating. Obviously having enough money to own a center-hall Colonial home and a BMW didn't mean you felt you knew how to be a perfect parent. Even upper-middle-class parents got called poo-poohead from time to time.

Based on these two pieces of information, I decided to change the positioning of the magazine. Instead of gearing it to *elite* parents, I would try to grab the bigger audience of fairly affluent yuppies, women like Hope Steadman from *thirtysomething*. And from now on we'd address more basic concerns parents had about their child's health and behavior—though in a more sophisticated way, befitting a more educated reader. (One of my favorite articles was "Babysitters from Hell: How to Spot One.")

# NOW FIND THE PULSE

An analysis of data is essential, but that's not all you must do to create your vision. You must also listen to your instincts to see if the vision *feels* right. Does it excite you, make you want to sing on your drive to work each morning? I always know I'm on the right track when I like my vision so much I feel as if I want to date it.

At *Child*, the data I got about what readers liked and didn't like made perfect sense to me on a visceral level. I was an educated, fairly sophisticated person, and yet I craved the most rudimentary parenting advice. You see, despite how competent and in control I was at the office, as a parent I was completely inexperienced and inept, feeling at times as if someone had handed me a newborn puma and told me to raise it until adulthood. I made a mess of the simplest of things. Once I forgot to wash my son's brand-new baby clothes before he wore them and when I took them off he had a little sticker on his bottom that said INSPECTED BY NO. 2. It seemed a glaring symbol of my lack of skill as a parent. A newly positioned

*Child* magazine, filled with solid advice, was exactly what *I* wanted to read.

## WRITE IT DOWN, EVEN IF IT MAKES YOU FEEL STUPID

Once you've worked out your vision, don't keep it in your head. Put it on paper, ideally in one succinct sentence. Though this seems like a third-grade exercise, writing it down will help you to crystallize it further and you'll have it there to refer back to constantly. It's easy to drift from your goal as you attempt to navigate the white waters of your workplace.

## A SPECIAL WARNING FOR GOOD GIRLS

When you're creating your vision, beware of the good-girl tendency toward earnestness. Good girls hope for a better world and, yes, that's admirable, but when you're involved with a product or service, you can't get weighed down with what *ought* to be. When I arrived at *McCall's*, it was suffering from a noble vision that wasn't in line with what everyday women wanted. After years of being a how-to magazine for mainstream women, it had been transformed into a repository for pieces like "Who Will be the First Woman President?" by William Safire and "Americans Need to Work Smarter, Not Harder" by Lester Thurow. Now, maybe in a perfect world everybody would stay abreast of Lester Thurow's thinking, but the *McCall's* subscribers wanted pieces like "Double Your Energy without Sleeping More," "Stay-Slim Ways to Eat Chocolate," and "Oprah's Secret Dream."

Don't let your vision be at the mercy of the Pollyanna factor. It should be based on what *can* be rather than what *should* be.

# WHY YOU NEED THE SLIM-FAST PLAN

Once you've got your vision, you need to figure out the key moves you must make to execute it—and that probably means putting it on a diet. As a good girl, your drive will be to do *everything*, but you must plan on a limited set of actions that you can actually pull off. Nancy Brinker, founding chairman of the Susan G. Komen Breast Cancer Foundation, the country's largest private funder of research dedicated solely to breast cancer and named in honor of Brinker's sister who died of the disease, follows what she calls "the three or four" rule. In building the Komen Foundation, she learned that you shouldn't try to concentrate on more than three or four major steps that relate to your overall plan. If you take on too many projects, you'll be unable to devote enough attention to any of them, and you'll end up looking like Janet Reno did that first year—playing endless hopscotch.

One way to stay focused is to pick several key words that sum up your goal. As Andrea Robinson began to revitalize Ultima II, she decided that their products would be "smart, fun, and sexy." It not only made it easy to assess ideas, but it also helped better define each product. When Ultima II developed a twelve-hour lipstick it became Lipsexxy. When they produced a fabulous mascara that plumped up lashes, it became, what else, but Falsies Mascara, with the slogan on the counter card: NOT SINCE THE PUSH-UP BRA HAS SOMETHING DONE SO MUCH FOR SO LITTLE.

# HOW TO GET A GUTSY PLAN OFF ITS DUFF

Now that you have your plan, you must turn it into a reality. Too many great missions get sucked into the quagmire of review and cogitation.

## Quick, Do Something

Management consultant Nancy Austin taught me that one trap many managers and executives fall into at this point is to assume that their first step should be big and bold—and that only slows down their pace. (I'm convinced good girls use this as an excuse for stalling.) Austin's philosophy is that you should get off the ground with a small but convincing success. In other words, think big but start small.

## Now Play It to the Max

You can get off the ground with a small step, but once you're rolling, you need to go for maximum impact. As you look at the three or four major goals that you've set as part of your vision, you have to think of how you can accomplish each in the boldest, gutsiest way possible. This is where you do the rule breaking, rule bending, and rule expanding I talked about in Chapter 3.

A few years ago, I worked with a terrific marketing consultant named Toni Maloney, president of the Maloney Group. What she taught me was that you take every idea and ask yourself how far you can run with it and how do you give it the "legs" to get there. For instance, part of the mission I

75

made for *McCall's* was to publish articles that would fully inform women about topics that had direct impact on their lives—like "The Politics of Breast Cancer" or "Why Working Mothers Are Losing Custody." Her advice: If you've got a great story in *McCall's*, don't just publish it. Find the senator who's in love with that particular issue and get him/her to give a press conference on it standing in a supermarket. Try to get the article entered in the *Congressional Record*.

One of Dr. Clyda Rent's plans for Mississippi University for Women was to promote the fabulous alumnae, such as Eudora Welty and O. Henry Prize founder Dr. Blanche Colton Williams, and other writers and literary types. Rent didn't settle for showcasing these women in a few brochures. She started the annual Eudora Welty Writers' Symposium as part of the Gala Fall Weekend. There's a Book and Author Dinner, at which the school hosts such nationally known writers as William Styron and John Grisham. She also named a building after Eudora Welty. Now that's playing it to the max.

# Be Gutsy Enough to Sacrifice

When you've made a list of the steps you must take to get to your destination, you're likely to discover that some of the projects your department has been diligently working on don't "fit" nicely with those steps. There is only one thing to do: kill them off. This isn't so hard with tasks that clearly aren't working, but it's far more difficult to take the ax to those that provide some short-term gain—like extra revenue or cachet or attention—even though they don't put you on a direct course to your goal. But you can't allow yourself to be seduced. Abandon anything that's superfluous.

After I'd gotten an understanding of the *McCall's* reader, it was clear that the kind of information she wanted most in the magazine were strategies for making smart choices about the areas of utmost concern in her life: her health, husband, kids, friends, clothes, money, etc. Ninety percent of the articles I commissioned fell into that category. But with the other ten percent I cheated a little. I felt we should also be doing some provocative pieces that would generate lots of publicity, even if they didn't generate much reader interest. One of the first of these kinds of features was a lingerie shoot with Marla Maples, who had recently split with boyfriend Donald Trump. The shoot was fabulous. Marla looked luscious in the clothes (though we had to stuff her bra with toilet paper), and much to our surprise, The Donald showed up, acting penitent. The icing on the cake was the fact that an "extra" photo of Trump feeding Marla grapes on the set was picked up by the Associated Press and it appeared in seventy national newspapers. What more could I hope for?

The problem: Our readers *didn't like* Marla Maples, and wrote in telling us to keep that good-for-nothin' husband stealer out of the magazine. I soon came to realize that even though these kinds of pieces took up a very small percentage of the magazine, they detracted from the mission of creating a magazine about the issues most dear to women. I'd told myself originally that readers could just skip over these pieces, but I realized they were probably dragging the whole product down, confusing readers about who we were.

Dr. Rent said that when she created her mission to be an inexpensive undergraduate school, she knew she was going to have to sacrifice trying to be competitive on a doctoral level. "These days you can't be all things to all people," she says. "You have to be a bistro rather than a cafeteria."

Be prepared for the fact that in the short term, sacrificing may cost you money. Laurie Ward says that she gets requests all the time to have her or one of her decorators do a traditional decorating job on a home or apartment. That entails having the decorator do all the shopping and oversee the workpeople, rather than simply providing a "plan" for the clients to execute themselves. "But we turn those jobs down," says Ward. "If we got into them, they'd divert us from our specialty."

# Hold Absolutely Everything up to Your Mission Statement

When you develop a new vision, it's likely that some of the habitual ways you do business in your department or your area won't facilitate that vision. And yet it may be difficult to notice it because they're so ingrained. It's essential to look at *all* your systems and evaluate whether any may be causing roadblocks for you.

When I went to *Working Woman*, I thought it looked as if it were trapped in the late seventies or early eighties, like a woman wearing a navy, man-tailored suit and sensible shoes. I wanted to make the magazine seem relevant for women's lives in the nineties. I was also concerned about advertisers' perception of the magazine. Many advertisers were under the assumption that *Working Woman* was a women's service magazine similar to *Self* and *New Woman*, rather than a publication filled primarily with career and management strategies.

I started making the graphics much livelier and the articles breezier. Then I set out to liven up the covers. For years the magazine had used models in business suits on the covers, twenty-three-year-old girls just out of Iowa, who knew so little about business that they probably thought that downsizing was something you had to do before a bathing suit photo shoot. The results seemed phony to me. I told the art director to find older, more experienced-looking models.

About five or six months into the job, I suddenly realized that I had accepted the model cover concept automatically—because that was how it had *always been done*. Yet using models only reinforced the idea that *Working Woman* wasn't really a business magazine. Could you imagine *Fortune* or *Forbes* hiring guys from the J. Crew catalog to pose in suits for their covers? From that point on I decided to use only successful, powerful women on the cover. I knew that "real people" wouldn't sell as well initially, but the magazine was primarily subscription driven. The new covers not only made the magazine seem much more energetic, but they suddenly fit with the mission.

# Remind Yourself of Your Vision Frequently

Take it out of your folder and reread it. It should be your reference point, a litmus test that you constantly hold ideas against. When *McCall's* won the Komen Foundation award for media coverage of breast cancer, I had the chance to go to Dallas for the presentation and meet Dr. Mary-Claire King, professor of epidemiology and genetics at the University of California at Berkeley, who is trying to find the gene for hereditary breast cancer. She told me that as she does her research she often asks herself, What is the reason I am asking this question? so that she never drifts from her mission.

# GETTING YOUR TROOPS ON BOARD

No matter how good your mission, no matter how sure you are of it, no matter how passionate you feel about it, you will never make it happen unless others become invested in it and are motivated to take the necessary steps.

The first thing you must do in order to galvanize them is to tell them what your vision is. It's amazing how often people keep those who work for them in the dark about both the destination and the clear directions for getting there. That doesn't mean you have to pass out copies of what you've written down, though that isn't such a terrible idea. In fact, that's exactly what Shirley DeLibero, executive director of New Jersey Transit, basically did. DeLibero runs one of the best transit systems in the country (the people in my office who commute from New Jersey love her). Her mission is printed on the back of every business card:

> To provide safe, reliable, convenient and cost-effective transit services with a skilled team of employees dedicated to our customer's needs and committed to excellence.

That's a fabulous idea to get everyone noticing, but in the age of information overload, sometimes a better way to do it is to . . .

## . . . SAY IT IN A SOUND BITE

As I read profile after profile of very successful women while I was editing *Working Woman*, I saw that one of the gutsy moves many of them made was to sum up their vision in a sound bite, much the way politicians and generals have been doing for centuries. Their goal becomes crystallized into one powerful line that is easy to grasp and remember.

How do you do that if you haven't been trained as an advertising copywriter?

Well, don't worry about it being cute and clever. In fact, it's far better to have people get what you mean instantly rather than have to spend time thinking about it. When Laurie Ward started her business, she ran the name Use-What-You-Have Interior Design by a number of friends, most of whom told her it was too wordy. And yet she felt that because her business was unique, it would be tremendously beneficial if people knew the moment they heard the name what it was all about. She went with it and feels that the name has played a powerful role in her success.

Jay Conger says that you shouldn't be afraid to be emotional with your vision statements. Touch people's need to belong, to feel like winners, to make a difference. Also, an unusual grammatical construction can stick in people's minds ("Ask not what your country . . ."). And it really helps if you can give them something to visualize.

When Nancy Brinker founded the Komen Foundation in 1982, it was around the time when the Vietnam War Memorial was being erected in Washington. Brinker discovered that a powerful sound bite and motivator was to tell people, "In a 10 year period, 58,000 lives were lost in Vietnam. In the same 10 year period, 330,000 women died of breast cancer. But there is no wall dedicated to them."

One of my favorite sound bite creators is Tina Brown, editor-in-chief of the *New Yorker* and formerly editor-in-chief of *Vanity Fair*. When she took over *Vanity Fair*, she said she wanted to go after "the disparate themes and elements that bind together a best-selling book—love, money, sex, dreams, death." That's not only visual, it's about as juicy as you can get. Who wouldn't want to execute a vision like that? When she went on to the *New Yorker*, she said she was creating a magazine for people who would "come for the relevance and stay for the daydream." Sound bite creators-in-training please take note: The word *dream* obviously has lots of impact.

# PUSHING THE RIGHT BUTTONS

A sound bite captures people's imagination. But in order for your employees to feel motivated to *fulfill* the mission, they have to have some kind of personal investment in it.

Nancy Brinker believes you need to appeal to the right brain, not the left brain. "Make people feel your mission personally. Often it helps to tell a story. I told the story of my sister over and over."

Certainly it will help if people feel there's something in it for them. That doesn't necessarily mean bonuses and perks, however. It may just be the thrill or prestige of being involved in working on a terrific project. In magazines, editors love to work on projects and articles that have stature, that have the potential for impact, because ultimately that stature rubs off on them.

# BEWARE OF THE NAYSAYERS

Practically the moment you get your vision out of your mouth, there will be a naysayer waiting eagerly to bully it and possibly knock it to the ground. Don't take it personally. Naysayers and doomsayers exist and thrive everywhere. Some of their favorite expressions are:

- "We tried that and it didn't work."
- "It will never fly."
- "Management hates that sort of stuff."

A good girl has a hard time handling naysayers. Her natural instinct is to foster cooperation and consensus and so she is likely to be bothered by their comments and let them influence her thinking and her actions. Of course, when you're developing your mission, it's critical to listen to people's concerns and reservations, but once you're sure of where you have to go, you can't let the sourpusses hamper you.

Your first goal with a naysayer is to try to convert her, to get her personally invested.

If you can't convert, then you must dilute the strength of the naysayer's grousing—otherwise it will plant doubts in the minds of your other employees. A terrific editor-in-chief once told me that she noticed at her magazine that over time a few of the people in each department developed a cynical attitude about what was possible in their areas. To combat this she often invited editors from other areas to certain departmental meetings, to give a breath of fresh air and offer up ideas that people in the department had long ago convinced themselves would "never work."

If a naysayer won't give up, you will have to get rid of her. It's not that she simply puts a damper on your meetings—or even on your day. She may, without your realizing it, be undermining all your efforts.

Not long after I got to *McCall's*, I hired an entertainment editor whose primary experience had been working at artsy publications, but she had lots of contacts in the entertainment business and seemed game to make a go of it at a more commercial publication like *McCall's*. Over time it became clear that she favored the more "intellectual" celebrities and looked down her nose at those best-selling crowd pleasers like Diana, Princess of Wales. She also began to develop the point of view that most celebrities didn't want to pose for *McCall's*. I'd say, "Why don't we see if we can get so-and-so," and she'd reply, "I'm sure she'd never do it." I'd just laugh and say, "Well, let's try, shall we?" Eventually, it seemed that more and more celebrities were turning us down. The excuse this editor usually gave was that celebrities thought our covers were too busy or "junky," because of the large cover lines and the photo insets we occasionally relied on. It was clear by the way she spoke that *she* wasn't so wild about the covers herself.

After she left, she was replaced by two editors working in tandem, and you know what? Gradually more and more celebrities seemed to want to be on the cover and no one complained about the look of our covers. Maybe it was pure coincidence, but I couldn't help but wonder if this editor's dislike of our covers and belief that no one would want to appear on them had come through in her conversations with agents. It was as if she had said, "We'd love Melanie for a cover, though I can't imagine she'd want to do it because there will be a photo of a pork roast and peach chutney right by her nose."

## WHEN IN DOUBT. . .

No matter how good your vision is, there will be times when you question it. Perhaps a setback forces you to doubt whether your plan is truly realistic. Or everything appears to be going smoothly but one day you whip your vision out of the folder and realize it sounds grandiose or worse, hokey. The best course is to sit for a couple of days and not make any decision to throw it away. You may simply be on a bumpy patch. If your doubts seem justified, there is only one step to take: Go back to the homework phase exploring strengths and weaknesses. Get input—and be willing to listen to what people say.

What you shouldn't do is share your raw doubts with anyone you work with. Certainly not your boss and not even your most trusted number-two person. You can indicate that you're doing some fact finding, but never show that you're worried about the course you've set.

One time I found myself wrestling with the vision I'd created at a magazine and I decided to share my doubts with several of the top people who worked for me. I told myself I needed their valuable input and the best way to get it was to be perfectly candid, but in hindsight I think that some residual good-girlism was directing me to find someone to agonize with. The trouble with baring your soul is that the people who work for you don't want to see you in any doubt because it automatically threatens their security. The women I confided in looked like children who had just finished watching the forest-fire scene in *Bambi*. In other words, you're on your own, girl.

# HOW A GUTSY GIRL STAGES A TURNAROUND

Sometimes developing a vision is about taking a good operation and making it relevant for the next ten years. Sometimes it's about giving a sluggish operation a jump start. And sometimes it's about taking a disaster and giving it CPR.

This is called doing a turnaround. It's an exhilarating experience and one of the fastest ways to make your mark. But it does mean being even gutsier in your approach than simply doing a jump start.

The basic trouble with having to do a turnaround is that all eyes are on you. Plus, though higher-ups realize on an intellectual level that you must get in there and study the situation before you make any moves, they seem to develop a terrible case of ants in the pants as you are finding your way. They want something to happen and they want it to happen fast.

There are three little tips I've learned over the years from watching women who have done turnarounds.

# I. Do Something Quickly That You Can Quantify

And better yet, something that improves the bottom line. When Shirley DeLibero started at New Jersey Transit, she picked three areas she could "deliver" on fairly quickly and announced them to the board of directors. One was operations and maintenance. When the service and on-time record improved quickly, those were factors everyone could *see*, plus, of course, they began to draw more riders.

# 2. Try Something Stunning That Gets Everyone Talking

I first heard this advice articulated by Pat Fili, now head of daytime programming for ABC, when we interviewed her for *Working Woman*. At the time she was head of programming for Lifetime and she'd been given the job of turning the cable network "for women" around. When she'd arrived at Lifetime, the channel carried reruns of long-forgotten network TV series like *MacGruder & Loud* and *Partners in Crime*, and plain drivel, including the insufferable *Attitudes*. The heat was on to do a quick turnaround. Fili, however, decided against making a lot of immediate changes because she needed to take the time to watch and study. But she also knew she had to do something to make it look like she was making a major impact. So she bought the rights to *The Days and Nights of Molly Dodd*. It generated lots of excitement, created the feeling that "Hey, this isn't the same old Lifetime anymore," but it didn't detract from her plan to watch and study.

One of the most dazzling buy-yourself-some-time moves is the one Christie Whitman, the governor of New Jersey, made on the day she took office. A few minutes into her inaugural speech she mentioned that during her campaign she had promised to put $1.4 billion of people's tax dollars back into their pockets by cutting taxes over the next three years, with the first cut coming in July. Then to everyone's shock she announced, "Why wait until the next fiscal year starts in July?" She asked her "partners in the legislature" to "enact a 5 percent income tax cut for every family in New Jersey effective January 1, 1994—17 days ago."

## 3. Call a Turnaround a Turnaround

Studies show that women tend to attribute their success to outside forces, and if *you* don't, other people will be quick to do that for you. If they can, they'll take the credit themselves, or they'll chalk it up to the marketplace, upper management, or luck. A friend of mine who turned around a magazine with an inventive change in the editorial learned that the circulation department was taking credit for the increase in renewals. Okay, maybe the clock radio sent to new subscribers played a role, but it wasn't the only factor. And yet the editor's efforts were overshadowed by the circulation department's forceful championing of its own efforts.

To prevent this you have to frame your turnaround in people's minds. Send out memos that keep people posted on the changes and their impact. When you talk to co-workers, use phrases like, "Thanks to our turnaround, we can . . ." And let the numbers get out there, too. If there's an 11 percent increase in customer sales, let everyone know.

As soon as DeLibero took over New Jersey Transit she began issuing quarterly reports to employees that she called *Vital Signs*. She gave plenty of facts and figures detailing the progress she was making.

# Strategy #3: A Gutsy Girl Does Only What's Essential

If you're a good girl, it goes without saying that you work hard for your money. After all, you want to prove yourself, get an A-plus on important projects, and please those who matter. The sure way to do that seems to be to work your tail off. Chances are there are plenty of lunch hours when you find yourself at your desk with a tuna salad and melba toast and plenty of evenings when you're the one who turns out the lights. You feel a lot of satisfaction (and yes, admit it, even a little smugness) in working harder than many of your colleagues, though sometimes that satisfaction turns to irritation when you realize that often you seem to get stuck with all the work. Just once you'd like to be heading out the door early on a Friday. But you know that in the long run you will be well rewarded for all your hard, hard work.

Well, I've got bad news. Despite what you've been encouraged to believe, all your hard work is no guarantee of rewards or success.

Okay, okay, just like me you've read all those profiles of top executives in *Fortune*, in which they play that one-upmanship game about the hours they put in—there's the 60-hour work-week and the 80-hour workweek and the 100-plus-hour workweek. Sure, some jobs do involve a mind-boggling number of hours, but I've come to see that many good girls get caught up in working long hours purely for work's sake, not because it's really necessary. They devote more attention to some projects than they have to, or handle certain assignments that they should actually give to someone else.

The trouble with working your tail off this way isn't simply that you end up without clean panty hose, a decent social life, a knowledge of twentieth-century fiction, or anything in your fridge other than expired low-fat yogurt. If you're creating endless make-work for yourself, you don't have time to focus on your gutsy-girl plan, on making something happen that's all yours—and that will make you a star.

A gutsy girl knows that the hours she clocks are no reflection of how good a job she's done. The secret is to stop trying to do *everything* and start concentrating only on the essential steps that will allow you to achieve your goal. Anything more is a waste of valuable time and energy.

# WHY GOOD GIRLS WORK HARDER THAN THEY SHOULD

At one of the magazines I edited, a department head hired a good girl who didn't know when to stop working. Whenever I asked to see a proposal she was putting together, the standard reply was, "I'm just finishing it up."

She might have been smart, she might have been talented, but it was almost impossible to tell because she suffered from can't-let-go-of-it-itis. Her case was fairly extreme and yet I've seen so many good girls experiencing varying degrees of this problem. Management consultant Nancy Hamlin, who specializes in gender issues, calls it the good girl "spin." Hamlin explains: "Women tend to work harder, do more research. They're always getting *one more* statistic."

Why do we work harder and longer than we have to? I once asked this question of a guy on my staff, who was often the first to hand in an assignment as the good girls in the department buffed theirs to death. "Men, by definition, are lazy," he said. "Women are trained to iron out wrinkles—every single inch of them."

According to psychologist Robin Post, it's a good girl's need for perfection that makes her overcook her projects or inhibits her from getting out of the gate with what matters most. A good girl was encouraged all through school to do things perfectly, and she saw that, unlike boys, she wasn't given any kind of dispensation for handing something in that was a little rough around the edges. She might have written a glorious, insightful book report, but if there was a hole in the paper from a pen eraser, she wouldn't get a perfect grade. To this day, she's afraid there will be a penalty if it isn't *just* right.

That's not to say that the work you hand in should be sloppy or incomplete, but if you spend too long on it, you could undermine yourself. Many ideas lose their freshness and energy if you overknead them. And, of course, bosses get supremely irritated if you are late with a project or never step out of your office with something to show for your efforts.

Another reason good girls work too hard on some tasks: there's a feeling of safety working with what's familiar. If it's a choice between snuggling up to a cozy, dog-eared report you've had in your possession for six weeks or tackling something new, you may choose to snuggle.

And last but hardly least, good girls work too hard simply because they think they ought to.

*The warning sign that you're working longer than you should on projects: You frequently hear yourself say:*

- "I'm putting the finishing touches on it."
- "I want to get it just right."
- "This is going to be really comprehensive."

# WHY GOOD GIRLS WORK ON WHAT THEY SHOULDN'T BE WORKING ON AT ALL

Perhaps an even greater sin than working too hard on something you *should* be working on is working for a single minute on something you should have given to someone else.

Delegation doesn't come naturally to many people, even the best of managers, but as a good girl you have your own unique reasons for resisting it.

First, there's that perfection thing happening again. You're fearful that if you turn part of a key assignment over to someone, he or she may screw up and make you look bad.

Your good-girl nature also wants you to be perceived as a nice, thoughtful person. You're afraid that people will be annoyed with you if you dump too much work on them, particularly grunt work. I know several good girls who empower their workers by delegating special projects to them but feel guilty turning over the crummy stuff, and thus end up doing *that* themselves.

And let's face it. You want to be thought of as Superwoman. If you delegate part of the work, you may no longer be viewed as the girl who can do it all.

*Warning sign that you are working on projects that you should be giving to someone else: You frequently hear yourself say:*

- "I was here all night."

# THE GUTSY GIRL'S THREE-STEP SYSTEM FOR DOING ONLY WHAT'S ESSENTIAL

Now that you have a sense of why you may fuss too much over your work or hang on to inappropriate tasks, it's time to move into action.

I don't want to sound braggy, but one of my best skills is the ability to concentrate only on what's essential. People sometimes ask me, "How do you do it all?" When I hear this question I occasionally feel a little surge of panic, wondering if the reason I have so much "extra" time is that there is a significant task that I'm not taking care of. Will I discover one day that all other human beings spend two hours a day doing something like draining their veins, and that my not doing so will result in the failure of my circulation at forty-five? But as the years go by and it becomes clearer that I'm not ignoring anything urgent, I see that the secret is dismissing the nonessential.

I can brag because once I was queen of the extraneous. I wanted to do it all so I could *say* I'd done it all. The first hint I had that this was a stupid approach was the summer before I went to work at *Glamour*. I had gotten a short-term job working in a political campaign, with responsibilities that included everything from doing advance work to spreading the word to the college crowd. One night some posters for a rally had to be painted and I got down on my hands and knees to do it myself. When I heard one of the higher-ups coming down the hall, I was sure he was going to walk into my office and canonize me. Instead he asked, "Can't you find some high school kids who can do that?"

I made gradual progress paring down my work, but it wasn't until I had a child that I was forced to be a master at it. Here are the three strategies that have worked for me.

# 1. Discover the Double To-Do List

There's not a woman alive who hasn't heard that she needs a to-do list. In fact, we became so obsessed with the concept that we turned the people who made Filofax into billionaires.

But simply having a daily to-do list won't get you anywhere. It will fill up with lots of housekeeping activities that good girls feel an obligation to stay on top of, like "order new computers" and "complete performance reviews." What you must have as well is a *master* to-do list that describes all the gutsy steps for executing your major goal. You then use this list to feed the daily one, making certain you always block off time for the important stuff.

In these crazy times, just taking care of the basics can consume all your time, but you absolutely have to make room for your big goals. Rebecca Matthias, president of Mother's Work, a chain of stores selling maternity clothing (which is estimated to do close to $60 million in sales this year) puts it a wonderful way: "You must drain the swamp at the same time you're fighting the alligators. That's the mark of a successful executive rather than just a manager."

# 2. Make It Snappy

Management consultant Nancy Austin likes to tell the story of a famous Canadian oil and gas wildcatter who on the eve of his retirement said, "It's so simple, it sounds stupid. It's amazing how few oil people really understand that you only find oil and gas when you drill wells." As Austin points out, "You can pray, plan, prospect, prepare, Filofax to the max, but the only way to make things happen, particularly big things, is to pick a starting point and drill. You know—Just Do It."

How do you train yourself to make it snappy if your instinct is continuously to cogitate, review, and be absolutely positively sure?

First, you need to recognize the myth that may be holding you back. Good girls try to make things perfect before releasing them because they think they *have* to be perfect. Wrong. In most instances, that's just not the case. You need to adopt the "half-baked cake approach" to ideas. I stole that phrase from Shirley DeLibero, executive director of New Jersey Transit. This is her philosophy: "I don't believe you always have to have a totally baked cake to go out there with. That doesn't mean I shoot from the hip, but much of the time it's important to just get started. You can always massage an idea along the way."

Rebecca Matthias says the same thing a slightly different way: "In our company, our approach is 'Don't tell us you're studying it, don't tell us you're working on it.' If the customer likes it, do it *now*. Find the middle ground between getting it right and letting it go. There's always room for refinement."

Her company motto: *Speed is life*.

One little electric cattle-prod trick you can use if you're in a stall is to schedule deadlines for yourself. And if you really want to be gutsy, send a memo to your boss saying when you expect to get a project in. Or—and this really takes nerve—schedule a meeting at which you'll *present* it in person.


## 3. Give Away the Grunt Work

I'm a ruthless delegator today, but it didn't come naturally to me. I often found myself buried under work that could easily have been done by others simply because I felt uncomfortable about telling another person to do it. I'm ashamed to admit that years ago I even took on certain secretarial jobs myself because I wanted to avoid seeing my assistant roll her eyes and sigh when I handed them to her.

Today I give away absolutely every bit of grunt work I can and save for myself the fun and important stuff of putting out the magazine. Maybe that's not "nice." But the twenty minutes it would take me to fill out the *Writer's Digest* questionnaire about what *Redbook* is looking for from writers is twenty minutes I can't devote to planning the August issue.

The way I got over my paralysis was to begin delegating a little bit at a time. As soon as I discovered the exhilarating sense of freedom and power it offered, the more I began to unload. It's not unlike hiring a weekly cleaning person for the first time. For years you tell yourself it really wouldn't be right to pay someone to do your own cleaning and, besides, housework gives you a chance to gather your thoughts. Once you finally get beyond that line of thinking and hire someone who makes your stove gleam and folds your underwear into little packets, you realize that you will never again be so stupid as to do it yourself.

The first step in delegating is figuring out what you should give away. It's basically quite simple: You give away anything you possibly can that doesn't necessitate your expertise and judgment. But don't go through the process once. Many of the most successful women I know say they *regularly* reflect on their responsibilities and determine what else they might be able to turn over to someone else. (If you haven't done a delegating review in more than a month, chances are you're doing something you shouldn't be.) When in doubt, ask yourself these questions:

- Will this activity really get me closer to my goal?
- Is this something someone else could do just as well?
- Would my boss mind if I gave this to someone else?
- Will anything really bad happen if the person screws up?

Even once you know there's work you can delegate, you may still feel uncomfortable letting go because of how people will react to being given "your" work, particularly the unpleasant stuff. The twenty-something generation, in particular, has a tendency to look miffed at being handed anything that doesn't seem to advance their careers. You may be wondering, in fact, how people react to *my* "dumping" techniques. There are two little strategies I use that appear to work for my staff (they're here, aren't they?):

- Always tell a subordinate that you have something for him to do rather than ask him if he can take it on. Asking not only allows the person to wiggle out of the task with one of those "Gee, I don't know. . . . I'm really swamped" comments, but it makes the task seem like something you're simply trying to ditch rather than a duty that's perfectly appropriate for this person.

- Whenever possible, package the task so that it seems critical or, even better, like a delicious opportunity. When I took over *Child* magazine, I discovered that there were only five staff members, a minuscule budget, and ninety pages to fill each issue. One cost-cutting idea I came up with: Each issue we'd fill four or five pages with a Q&A format interview with a different parenting expert. That way we'd end up with what amounted to an "article" by a hotshot in the field, but it wouldn't cost us anything. Because we were so short staffed, I'd have to do the interview myself and—uh-oh—my assistant would have to transcribe it. The reason I say uh-oh is that she hated grunt work and loved to punish me with sullenness for giving it to her. I'd certainly pay the price for this. Then I had a little brainstorm. I went out to her desk and announced to her that I was giving her her own column in the magazine. Each month I would help her generate the questions and then she would interview the expert, transcribe the tapes, edit down the results and get the by-line. She was delirious with joy. Each month I'd allow myself a sneaky laugh as I watched her transcribe for hours at her desk in what seemed like a state of Nirvana.

# DON'T WORRY IF YOUR PEERS DESPISE YOU

There is a small downside to learning to focus on only what's essential. Your peers may hate you for it. They will make little digs about the fact that you seem to be one step ahead of the game and not buried under a pile of paperwork, turning it into a negative rather than a positive. A friend of mine who was a master delegator overheard someone call her the Teflon Lady because "nothing sticks to her desk." Ignore their comments and realize that what your boss is looking at are the results you deliver.

# EVERYTHING YOU NEED TO KNOW ABOUT PROCRASTINATION BUT NEVER GOT AROUND TO ASKING

It may seem odd suddenly to raise the subject of procrastination. I've been talking about how hard and long good girls work, so why would I now launch into the topic of not doing any work at all?

Well, the good girl's dirty little secret is that she *does* procrastinate, sometimes sitting on a project until the absolute last minute. And, interestingly, the reason she does this may be the same behind why she works too hard on other things. Psychologist Post, who has seen procrastination dog many successful women she counsels, says, "In many cases procrastination has to do with a fear of not being perfect or not getting it right." Just as this fear may prevent a good girl from letting go of a project, it can also hinder her from even getting started.

The problem fuels itself. "Each day you procrastinate, the issue takes on a greater and greater weight," says Post. In other words what seemed on Tuesday like a mildly difficult task, by Friday has begun to seem like bone surgery without anesthesia—and thus you're even more apt to put it off.

I was the world's most consistent procrastinator in my twenties, someone who had to pull all-nighters at *Glamour* just to write pieces like "How Not to Get a Single Pimple This Summer" because I hadn't left enough time. It would take me months to complete major articles, and though I could see the negative effect it was having on my career, I just couldn't change.

It amuses me to reread these words now because they seem to be written about another human being. I never procrastinate today; in fact, I always prepare early for everything. There are two things that helped me change my ways.

# 1. I Learned to Play Cut the Salami

To help me get over my procrastination problem, I wrote several pieces on the subject, and from a time-management expert named Edwin Bliss I learned a technique that made all the difference. It's called "the salami technique." His theory, and there are variations on this theme by other time-management experts, is that any big task staring you in the face is similar to a giant hunk of salami—it's very unappetizing to look at. However, if you cut the salami into thin slices, it is much more appealing; in fact it will look quite attractive on your creamy white Italian platter.

The same principle applies to work projects. If you stall on a project and then attempt to do it all at once, it will become a monster. But if you cut it down into manageable pieces, the whole project will look easier.

Let's say your boss asks you to give her some ideas for line extensions of the product your division is responsible for. This kind of project has a big sprawling feel to it—and you keep hoping for a couple of open days on your calendar to wrestle it to the ground.

With the salami technique you don't wait for a few free days. Instead, you begin immediately and do a little at a time. Over the years I've found that for me, the smaller I make the steps the better—I guess you could say I like my salami sliced really thin. I've also found that a sneaky and very effective trick is to assign the first step or two to a person on my staff, and then I don't have to be the one who jumps into the pool first. For instance, if I were asked by my boss to come up with line extension ideas, I might, as the first step or slice, send a memo asking my staff to give me *their* ideas; step two would be reading over their comments. Each step requires very little effort on my part and yet I will have nicely managed to get the ball rolling. From there I might jot down my own thoughts, and next do a rough outline. The beauty of this kind of approach is that not only are the individual steps easy, but each one actually generates the next.

# 2. I Learned to Savor the Pleasure of Not Being Late

As I said earlier, procrastinating is a bit like bone surgery without anesthesia. There's the dread. And the agonizing. And the pain. You find yourself one night frantically going through papers, scribbling notes at eighty-five miles an hour, hating yourself. I'd be cocky as hell for days as I procrastinated, but the night before something was due I'd start whimpering.

Once I started using the salami technique, I discovered the amazing serenity and relief that comes from early preparation. There I'd be with three days before the deadline and all I'd have to do is tie up a few loose ends. Since then I've learned to conjure up that feeling whenever I'm looking at a project. I let myself think of how good I will feel if I get an early start—and how pathetically miserable I'll be if I don't. It's a little behavior modification in the hands of an amateur but it has worked beautifully.

## HOW TO USE YOUR TIME BRILLIANTLY

Even once you've learned to delegate the projects that aren't essential and get momentum going on what matters, you can still run into trouble making your gutsy plan a reality if you don't know how to use your time well. Here's what can happen:

You schedule your calendar so you have time for both the basics and the big-picture stuff. But then things go a little crazy. Somebody complains, somebody resigns, a project gets derailed, and your day is shot. When your days get disrupted this way, there's an interesting phenomenon that takes hold: The housekeeping stuff somehow manages to get done. It almost has a life of its own, nudged along by the system (the accounting department calls and reminds you about the paperwork on the new computers). The big-picture stuff, however, can get endlessly postponed.

These days, everyone has difficulty making time for what matters. Peter Vaill, a professor of management at George Washington University, describes the world of work today as "permanent white water." Most people, he says, "have this fantasy that stability is the norm and that chaos is the exception. After the new person comes onboard, after the computer is debugged, once we move to the new building, things will settle down. That's just a dream we have."

Good girls have their own brand of trouble with their time because everybody wants some of it. People are always asking for help, popping in uninvited to talk. You may go through the day with a sense of never having enough time or of time getting away from you.

That's the wrong perspective. You have to be bold and gutsy about your time, treat it like a dog in obedience school—it must conform to your needs, follow your commands. If you don't constantly show that you're the master, it will take a juicy bite out of your thigh.

## Make Time for What Matters Most

The only way you can guarantee that your big-goal time is not taken from you is to make it unassailable. One strategy is to schedule it for when you're out of the office. Some executives say they use airplane flights this way.

What I do is close my door for an hour a day (and before I had a door I actually used to find quiet places in the building or even the cafeteria).

It took me a while to feel nervy enough to do this on a regular basis—not only because good girls have a hard time saying no to people, but because we also have a fear of looking like we're being naughty, something we assume that a closed door may suggest.

The idea of closing your door for priority work became popular with time-management experts during the seventies but lately it's faced some criticism. In his research on how managers use their time, John Kotter, Konosuke Matsushita professor of leadership at the Harvard Business School, found that they are extremely fluid, responding constantly to interruptions and problems. A closed door, he theorizes, disrupts fluidity. But I believe that if you don't do it, you will spend your day like a ricocheting bullet. A few words of caution, however:

- Your closed-door time should never be first thing in the morning because that's when people need to see you with problems from the afternoon before.
- It should be roughly the same time every day so people come to recognize it for what it is rather than think you're sleeping off a hangover or having a nasty fight with your husband or boyfriend on the phone.
- It shouldn't be too long (about an hour is good), or it will annoy the hell out of people.
- Your boss has to be comfortable with it—some bosses hate it when subordinates close their doors, and if that's the case, don't.

One other option I'm fond of: the half-closed door. It shows you're alive and working but discourages those with less-than-urgent business.

# Banish the Time Intruders

Each day we're all bombarded by time intruders. Sometimes time intruders are inanimate—traffic jams, broken copy machines—but 85 percent of the time they're other human beings. That's why it's so hard for good girls to handle them. Our instinct for being nice prevents us from booting these people out of our office or saying no to their requests for help they should be getting elsewhere.

This is not to say that everyone who pops into your office and asks, "Gotta minute?" is a time waster. Studies have shown that effective managers have frequent interruptions from staff members and often these interruptions provide essential information. Sometimes, in fact, the person doesn't even realize that a piece of info is important, and you stumble upon it during a casual discussion. If you are constantly finding ways to limit their access to you, or shoo them out of your office, you can end up out of the loop.

On the other hand, people will often eat up far more of a good girl's time than necessary. You have to know how to manage your time with them and not give in to your tendency to be polite and nurturing.

Try these strategies:

- Stop being a good listener about personal issues. If you let them, people will turn you into their in-office therapist, confessing to you that their boyfriend says he can't relate to them because they've never been in a twelve-step program or describing in detail their irritable bowel syndrome. Avoid therapist behavior, such as very relaxed body language and expressions like "Hmmmmm."
- When someone does drop by your office, set a time

frame around the encounter. "I have a meeting at one P.M., but I can take ten minutes now."

- If the person has made his or her point and now is into chitchat, get up gradually (first sitting on the arm of the chair instead of in it) and then slowly ease your way toward the door.
- Don't *add* anything to the conversation. You have to resist the urge that good girls have—even with a nowhere conversation—to ask a question or pleasantly affirm what the person is saying. Every time you say, "Really. That's amazing," you are guaranteed to lose a minimum of five more minutes of your time.

## Be a Ballbuster with Paperwork

Just as people will take advantage of a good girl's time, so will paperwork. Some of the good girls on my staff seem to be victims of their paperwork, as if they were being ordered around by a big bully who didn't believe in ever letting them take a break. You have to be gutsy with your paperwork, treat it as if you're the boss and it's always at your beck and call.

When I was writing pieces on time management, I read thousands of tips on paper management but there were two that really worked beautifully—and unlike so many time-management techniques, these have *continued* to work over the years.

The first is never to handle a piece of paper more than once. This is a classic piece of advice from time-management guru Alan Lakein, whom I interviewed near the beginning of my career (he returned my call from an airport, between planes, reinforcing the idea that he never wasted a moment). As soon as you touch a piece of paper, make a decision about what to do with it—whether it's file it, pass it on, work on it, or destroy it—and then do just that.

The second is to categorize your work pile. I used to have one monolithic work pile. Some days it was smaller than others, but I never seemed to get to the bottom of it. When new material hit my desk, it would go right on the top of my inbox, and sometime during the day I'd try to sort through and find the most important stuff. It wouldn't be unusual for me to miss some critical memo because it had been pushed down to the bottom, left to mate with an announcement of a new Smokenders' program available to employees.

Today, everything that comes into my office is put into one of five different-colored folders, depending on its priority and what kind of work it involves. I use a car service to get back and forth to the office, and having the folders makes it really simple for me to attack work in the car. I keep a pad of Post-its, and since I don't handle a piece of paper more than once (I swear, Mr. Lakein), each piece I work on is then marked with a command for my assistant. The combination of these two techniques (classifying and only handling things once) is a great system for good girls because it also forces you into the role of active delegator.

# NEVER APPEAR AT THE MERCY OF YOUR TIME (OR WHAT I LEARNED THE WEEK I HAD LUNCH WITH HILLARY CLINTON AND SUSAN POWTER)

Because it's important to a good girl to be perceived as a hard worker, she never minds (in fact she *likes* it) if someone catches her looking a little frantic: riffling through papers, dashing down the hall with her hair flying, lugging home a huge pile of work on Friday afternoon. Being in overdrive, she believes, shows everyone that she not only has lots to do but is getting it done.

Though it's important to be perceived as energetic, acting frazzled or short on time actually creates the impression that you aren't under control, and that calamity is waiting just around the corner to ambush you. It makes bosses reluctant to turn more responsibility over to you and it makes co-workers and subordinates as anxious as passengers on a bumpy 747.

A few months ago, I got to see the two best living examples of the Frazzled and Unfrazzled styles. It just so happened that in one week I went to luncheons for weight-loss maven Susan ("Only fat can make you fat") Powter and First Lady Hillary Rodham Clinton.

I hosted the lunch for diet guru Susan Powter in the executive dining room so that my editors could meet her. We had just done one of the first major pieces about her in a national magazine. She burst off the elevator going eighty miles an hour, and she maintained that speed for the next two hours. Though the message she perpetuates is that women must end their insane approach to food, she never touched her meal, making the rest of us feel like gluttons. She talked almost nonstop in something very close to a bark, never asked anyone a question, and gestured wildly with her arms, at the same speed as a helicopter's rotor. (I imagined myself calling security to announce that we had two or three heads rolling around the floor.)

By 2:00 P.M. everyone on my staff looked like they'd been forced to do two hours' worth of step aerobics while watching a televangelist speak in Pentecostal tongues.

A few days later was a luncheon for magazine editors in Washington with the First Lady. Now if anyone had the right to seem frazzled and short on time, she did (she was in the midst of promoting the Clinton health reform plan), but there was a serene quality about her. She glided into the room, took your hand slowly and carefully, and gazed into your eyes as if the only thing she wanted to be doing at that moment was looking at you. Perhaps, I thought, she'd learned a little something about Zen during a session on alternative medicine. It was a delicious experience and one that left me wanting to eat out of her hand. It was very similar to the calm, steady approach she used during her press conference on her commodities trading, which everyone, including Rush Limbaugh, admitted was a triumph.

The lesson: Yes, time is short, but never look as if it's got the best of you. Take a deep breath, savor the moment, and show that you're calm and in control.

# GO AHEAD, DARE TO TAKE A SHORTCUT

Admit it. When you were in college you saw other kids studying with Cliffs Notes rather than reading the whole book, but you wouldn't even consider it. Taking a shortcut was almost as bad as cheating. That kind of thinking has probably stayed with you. As a good girl, you believe that if you shave anything off your workload it will somehow catch up with you. A perfect example from my own life: When I was an articles editor I had to read the unsolicited manuscripts that came in through the mail. I soon discovered that the first page alone was always enough to tell me if the piece was any good, but I dutifully would read the entire article. I had this vague sense that someone, perhaps the same enforcement team that monitored the improper removal of those DO NOT REMOVE tags from pillows, would discover that there were no fingerprints on the last nine pages and I would be slapped with a penalty.

Well, there are no penalties for good shortcuts. In fact, they can be your salvation on many occasions. Try using Post-its instead of writing memos, skimming the table of contents of your trade publications and journals instead of reading all the articles, writing notes back to people directly on the memos they send you.

One of my favorite gutsy-girl shortcuts is never taking notes at meetings. I learned this technique from a Kikuyu guide I had on safari in Kenya during my single years. Everyone in our group had arrived with cameras with telephoto lenses, which they rarely took away from their faces. They looked perfectly silly. I asked the guide once if he ever took photographs of the animals and he said, "The Kikuyu takes the picture in his own mind." Considering his words later, I realized that I was so busy taking pictures myself, adjusting the f-stop and the focus, that I wasn't absorbing the raw beauty of the Kenyan landscape. That lesson not only led me to abandon my camera on my travels, but down the road it also inspired me to examine the copious notes I took at meetings. Not only did I rarely get around to consulting the notes (for starters I couldn't read them), but I'd be so busy organizing the notes and keeping pace with the speaker that I didn't fully absorb the message. Now, I listen and pick the key points to remember.

# FIVE WORDS WINNERS NEVER SAY

When I got the job as editor-in-chief of *Child* with a seven-month-old baby at home, I had made a commitment to myself to leave at 5:00 every day. I soon saw that in order to do that I was going to have to be very inventive about how I used my time.

During those first weeks people constantly popped into my office with requests or handed me material to evaluate. I took it all into my little hands and promised, "I'll get back to you." What's ironic about this approach is that there's an illusion that it buys you time when it actually uses up *more* time. You're forcing yourself to consider the request not once, but every time it stares at you from your in-box. Within several days I knew that I'd be at the office until 9:00 every night if I stayed with this approach. I could see that I would have to banish the phrase, "I'll get back to you" from my repertoire and make decisions on the spot.

Initially, making an instant decision seems scary. But if you're skilled at your job and on top of your responsibilities, there's every reason you should be able to decide something instantaneously—unless you have to look up numbers or get an okay from higher up. The reason we so often say, "I'll get back to you" isn't that we don't know the answer but because we've gotten into the habit of delaying a response (it's like saying, "ummmmm" when we speak), or we're doing it so we don't have to hurt anyone's feelings on the spot.

Begin by making instant decisions on issues that you could later change your mind on if necessary. Your paperwork will drop by about 30 percent. Anyone who works for you will love it because most employees want an answer and it drives them insane to wait. And, you will seem incredibly decisive to anyone around you.

# THE BEST LESSON DR. RUTH TAUGHT ME

When I was the executive editor in charge of articles at *Mademoiselle*, Dr. Ruth Westheimer was a frequent contributor who conducted roundtables for us with young women on the topic of sex. I spent time with her before the roundtables, going over the questions and details, and I discovered that she is every bit as dynamic and wonderful in person as she is on talk shows. It would be nice if I could admit that she taught me about some exotic sexual techniques guaranteed to keep a marriage rated R for fifty years, but that's not the case. What I learned isn't very sexy and yet it's served me well.

Every time Dr. Ruth came to the *Mademoiselle* offices to conduct a roundtable in our showroom, she'd say, "Kate, I need to tek a vew minoots alone inn your ahfeece." She'd then spend ten minutes eating a sandwich at my desk with the door closed. At the time I was struck mostly by the fact that her feet didn't touch the floor as she ate, but years later something else occurred to me. What she was doing was creating a little pocket of peace and quiet for herself—and I'm sure it helped refresh and energize her. I believe she was the first woman I ever saw give herself permission to do that during a workday.

I try to do that for myself now, by sneaking off to have lunch by myself or even getting a massage. That's a hard thing for good girls to do because we feel that it's a sign of laziness to play. But a break ends up in the long run making you more productive. Give yourself permission.

# CHAPTER SIX

# Strategy #4: A Gutsy Girl Doesn't Worry Whether People Like Her

> The bottom line root of all my problems is I had a fear of not being liked. . . . I ended up ruling my life based upon what other people wanted me to do. . . . Like most women, I think I was raised with this disease to please. . . . It kept me from really being the person that I think I was born to be.

If you had to guess who made the above statement, you just might assume it was a guest on *Sally Jessy Raphael* or *Oprah*, bemoaning why life hadn't gone her way. But these words actually came from Oprah herself. Oprah Winfrey, whose '93–94 income was estimated at $105 million. What she seemed to be saying was that she could have done even more with her life if she hadn't been concerned with taking care of other people's needs at the expense of her own.

Now, it boggles my mind to imagine Oprah accomplishing anything more than she already has, but who knows? Maybe she could have been a star talk-show host, an Oscar-nominated actress, an outstanding businesswoman, *and* a pediatric neurosurgeon if she hadn't been such a pleaser. But regardless, I think every good girl can relate to her words, particularly that phrase "disease to please."

Why can pleasing people be seen as a disease? Because no matter how much it might benefit anyone else, it can impair your own vitality and ability to function well.

The drive to please starts early. Every woman can look back and see how she was encouraged to be a pleaser, and yet it's so interwoven into the fabric of who we are, we're not aware of all the millions of small ways it takes hold.

Consider this fascinating nugget: In a study done recently by a Loyola University-Chicago marketing expert, it was found that by the age of three, many American girls have already learned the basics of such typically female adult rituals as gift-buying and party-giving.

"In our culture, women are primarily responsible for most of the gift- and party-giving," says study coauthor Mary Ann McGrath, Ph.D., an associate professor of marketing at Loyola. "Through this study, we've found that girls are taught these roles, consciously or unconsciously, much earlier than we realized."

In describing reasons for giving birthday gifts, boys were much more likely to give pragmatic answers, while girls were generally more altruistic and tended to focus on the pleasure experienced by both the giver and the recipient. One typical girl's response was, "It's nice to give presents . . . then they get to have lots of toys."

Women today have become more aware of how the need to please can dominate our personal lives, especially with our boyfriends and spouses. There have been countless books and articles on how we assume the "caretaker" role in relationships, and we've learned that it's enormously healthy to learn to share that job.

We might not be aware, however, of how it takes hold at

work. That "please be nice" message has burrowed in pretty deep by this point and it may affect how you relate to your boss, your peers, and your subordinates. Management consultant Judy Markus, who as head of Communication Dynamics advises hundreds of clients each year, makes this observation: "Women want to walk out of a room of business associates and feel liked by everyone in that room."

It may seem up until now that I'm implying that trying to please people and make them like you isn't a worthwhile goal. But that's not the case at all.

"The desire to please others is a tremendously positive one," says Judith Jordan, Ph.D., a psychologist and coauthor of *Women's Growth in Connection.* "It helps knit society together."

It's also an essential part of our nature as females, though excuse me for paraphrasing Marilyn Quayle. According to Jean Baker Miller, the founder of the Stone Center for Research on Women at Wellesley, "Women mature in the context of relationship, contrary to the male model of autonomy and separation." Whereas little boys must partially break away from their mothers in order to shape their identity, girls are able to form a tighter bond. Miller says that girls and women thrive in relationships and for women the apex of development is to "weave themselves zestfully into a web of strong relationships that they experience as empowering, activating, honest, and close." Our sense of self rests on our ability to do that.

And though this sounds far less noble, and even downright mercenary, career success depends to a large degree on having the right people like you and knowing how to please them. (More about this later.)

The trouble starts when your need to please inhibits your ability to get your job done and advance your gutsy-girl plan. Playing the pleaser can cut into your time—you don't take care of your priorities because you are busy holding someone's hand or bailing them out. One theory suggests that one factor that may limit female college professors' ability to "publish," and thus win tenure, is the amount of time they spend mentoring, nurturing, and coordinating activities with students.

Even if you're not giving too much of your time, a desire to be liked can simply create a perception of you that undermines your efforts. You come across as needy and dependent (think Sally Field at the Academy Awards). And ultimately that can take away your control.

"When your sense of self-worth is dependent on whether other people like you, you end up giving your power to them," says Denver psychologist Robin Post, who counsels many career women she sees caught in the pleaser role. Over time your boss realizes that your need to be liked means you won't make a fuss over a puny raise, your peers realize that it means you won't speak up if your turf is invaded, and your secretary realizes it means you won't challenge her when she takes her fifth mental-health day. You're at their mercy.

# FIRST AID FOR THE DISEASE TO PLEASE

So how can you possibly treat the disease to please? Certainly fourteen days of amoxicillin and some cold compresses to the head aren't going to knock out something that's this ingrained.

Probably the single thing that helped me overcome the need to be the most popular girl at work was the realization that it just couldn't be done. Think back to high school for a minute. One of the phrases used about popular kids is, "Everyone loves her." In other words, back then it seemed that if you tried hard enough, it was within the realm of possibility to enchant each and every kid in your class.

But as people age, they get more complex, develop different

needs and lots of emotional baggage. Winning them over is no longer as simple as passing them in the corridor and announcing, "I love your hair like that." No matter how hard you try, some people just won't like you.

"When someone doesn't like you in your company, it might be because of something you've done, but it could just as easily be due to a factor out of your control," says Post. "They dislike you simply because you remind them of their mother."

Besides, even the people who like you one moment may not the next if your career really starts to barrel along and theirs doesn't. Management consultant Kay Peters of New York City has this philosophy: "If you are successful, there will be at least several people in your organization who don't like you simply due to that fact, and if you're also good looking they will hate your guts."

# HOW TO SAY NO—AND REALLY MEAN IT

Even when you change your own mind-set about being the pleaser, it will take other people a while to catch on. Having you in that role may have suited them just fine, especially if it's meant that they could count on you to take care of some of their business—finish up their projects, tidy up their messes, listen to them rant or rave.

A big part of giving up the pleaser role is learning how to say no.

You can't say no to everything you don't like. It's your boss's right to dump some of the work on you, and in many cases, certain projects that at first glance might seem nasty could help you develop an invaluable expertise or specialty or else expose you to key people in the organization. When I was working as a feature writer at *Glamour*, one of the editors walked over to my desk one day at 4:49, as she was leaving to catch the 5:10 commuter train to Long Island, tossed a manu-script on my desk, and asked me to edit it for her. I mumbled a feeble "okay" and watched in annoyance as the tail of her red coat flicked in the doorway. My job didn't include editing (in fact, I'd never even edited an article) and it was obvious that the only reason I was being given this assignment was that it was due the next day and the editor had other things to take care of.

But as I began to work on the article, I discovered how thrilling it was to edit someone's words, to scratch and rephrase and cut and paste. I also realized that I was holding a ticket in my hands. This was what I could use to launch my-self up to another level. Dump all you want, I thought, and she did. Over the next few months I edited many articles, and seven months later I got a job as a senior editor at another magazine because I'd had a crash course in the process of line editing.

What you want to avoid, if possible, are the projects that are tickets to nowhere. Here's the best approach:

- Give yourself the stomach test. When an added responsi-bility is a real loser, one that will do nothing for your ca-reer and only make you rue the day you ever accepted it, you will experience a dull squeezing feeling in your stomach. This is your warning that you must try to get out of it.
- Offer an excuse that's tied to one of your key responsibil-ities—and make it short and sweet. For instance, let's say the human resources director has just asked you to be on the relocation committee. Your response: "I'm flattered you asked, but I have to say no. I'm supervising the sales conference and I must devote all my efforts to making that a success."
- Never say maybe. *Maybe* is unfortunately one of a good

girl's favorite words. You really mean no, but over time you've come to believe that maybe just sounds nicer. But the person doing the asking reads maybe as a possible yes, and will continue to hound you. When you do finally say no, she will be immensely irritated for having been led down the primrose path.

# TWO "PLEASER" HABITS YOU DON'T KNOW YOU HAVE

Okay, you're beginning to reform your pleaser style. But you may be looking like a pleaser even when you have no intention of being one. Good girls use two types of body language that can make them seem "too nice":

- The smile. Studies repeatedly show that women smile more than men. There are plenty of times when a smile will work for you. But not all the time. Alan Mazur, a professor at Syracuse University and an expert on body language, says that at the wrong moment a smile can signal you're a pushover.

  "When we're nervous, we look for ways to relieve our anxiety," says Dr. Mazur. "One way is through affiliative behavior, like smiling. It can be a way to form a connection. But in a business setting the other person can begin to pick up, on an intuitive level, that the smile means you're frightened, obsequious, and intimidatable."

  My speech coach, New York–based communications consultant Pam Zarit, says that many of the women she coaches come in prepared to smile their way through everything they say. Her advice is to use a smile sparingly, when you really need it. "When you plaster a smile on your face, you have no place else to go."

- The head nod. If you watch a meeting of men and women, you'll notice that women do most of the nodding. When *McCall's* ran a roundtable of the seven female U.S. Senators in Washington, I was struck by how much the senators nodded as their peers spoke, showing their respect and support for their colleagues' words.

  But nodding can get you into trouble. It can make you look compliant, easy to please. It can also give away more than you'd planned to reveal. Sometimes we nod purely out of habit, which can totally confuse our listeners. Management consultant Nancy Austin told me that she was once in a meeting with a woman who was asked if she could cut more money from her budget. The woman forcefully defended her budget and said she couldn't—but nodded her head throughout her statement. It was the old "your lips say no but your body's saying yes."

## THE GUY SECRET OF NEVER TAKING THINGS PERSONALLY

The need to be liked and the desire to please are part of a bigger issue for good girls on the job: the driving inclination to take things personally. It's probably hard for you at times not to relate what happens back to yourself. If the boss is huddled behind closed doors, if someone doesn't return a call, if someone makes a curt remark, you may immediately wonder, What did I do?

Management consultant Nancy Hamlin, who is president of Hamlin Associates, says she sees this frequently in women she works with and feels it saps their energy and attention. She tries to encourage them to look at things in a bigger context.

Some people just happen to be brusque or frequently preoccupied, and if you factor that in, you realize that their behavior has nothing to do with you.

Of course, it's tougher not to personalize things when they do relate directly back to you, when, for instance, a project you've been working on gets a lukewarm response. This is where women get into what career strategist Dr. Adele Scheele calls women's "blame yourself" mind-set. Whereas men have a brilliant way of detaching themselves when things don't go their way, a good girl experiences a tidal wave of angst.

New York City management consultant Karen Berg said that she recently posed this scenario to a smart, dynamic, thirty-something woman she worked with: "You and a male colleague make a presentation to a group of clients. At the end, the clients say that they think your approach doesn't work for them. You agree to come back with some new ideas. As you and the male colleague leave the room, what are you each thinking?"

"That's easy," said the woman. "He'd be blaming the clients. I'd be blaming myself."

In a study by the Center for Creative Leadership (CCL), executives were asked to respond to the statement, "Tell me about a time you tried something and failed." All of the women responded in detail, but half of the men said they could not come up with a single example. "It's likely that both men and women make the same number of mistakes," notes CCL director of leadership technologies Ellen Van Velsor, "but women agonize more over them."

Countless studies on attribution have revealed that men tend to blame outside forces for their setbacks, whereas women assume the problem lies totally with them. Is it any wonder? Dr. Myra Sadker and Dr. David Sadker found in their research on schoolkids that teachers often explained away boys' poor performance ("Maybe you were tired," or "Maybe you didn't get enough sleep"), while rarely offering the same kind of out for girls.

Now it would be nice if you could just say to yourself, I'm not going to let it bug me anymore, but that's a tad unrealistic. One gutsy girl I know who runs a major division in a company says that she realizes she can't change years of ingrained behavior so she allows herself five minutes of self-flagellation and then she moves on.

What *men* do so well is find their own special words to position any setback. It's something society seems to program them to do. My brother Rick told me the most enlightening tidbit the other day. He was shopping for a new suit and after trying on a few jackets, it became clear that because he'd gained a few pounds he wasn't going to have much luck with a standard cut. The salesman looked at him with a smile and said, "I think you'd do better with the *executive* fit."

Now when women gain weight we have to head for stores like Forgotten Woman. But guys get the *executive* fit.

They play the same kind of word game with setbacks. For instance, they never say, "My idea got shot down." They say, "We decided to go in another direction." Try this wonderful re-labeling game yourself.

What works for me, I've discovered, is to go on an information-gathering mission.

I learned this strategy during a night of newsstand hell after I'd been at *Child* magazine for about seven months. My first four covers had sold really well on the newsstand, and I was happy to know there were some basic principles for success. But one day, to my dismay, a piece of paper arrived from Circulation indicating that sales estimates for the last issue were being revised significantly downward and that projections for the most recent issue were very low.

That night I couldn't stand thinking about the situation any longer so I took the ten previous covers of *Child*, laid them on my bed, and began trying to analyze what worked and what didn't. Did girls sell better than boys? Were cute clothes better than trendy ones? Did a little drool on the mouth turn off the buyer or endear her? Did a big behavior line on top, like HOW TO TAME A TEMPER TANTRUM, help sell better than a health one, like ARE VEGETABLES SAFE FOR KIDS? No clear pattern was emerging yet, but at least my juices were flowing, and I knew that I'd eventually figure it out. Also, the research had given me something to do other than agonize.

The next day, I arrived at my office feeling galvanized. Do you know what I discovered? That there'd been a typo in the circulation news I'd gotten and that the two covers were actually projecting to sell very high. Fantastic news, but I swear that my greatest relief was not from getting the revised sales information. What delighted me was that I had finally found a way to deal with bad news: Get more information.

You may be reluctant, as good girls often are, to poke around for fear of what you'll turn up. There's probably a sense that the facts will confirm your worst nightmares or be even worse than you imagined. A good-girl friend of mine told me that after a big screwup she was afraid that if she looked too deeply she would find a piece of paper that said, *It's all your fault, babe.*

But what often happens when you start to investigate is that you learn there were other forces at work. And even if you are culpable, the facts you get are the first step to solving the problem. Besides, all the busywork does a beautiful job of preventing you from agonizing.

## LEARNING TO LOVE CRITICISM

An unavoidable part of your job is having your boss criticize your work at times. No matter how talented and capable you are, there will be instances when you screw up, go down the wrong road, or simply handle a problem in a way that may be perfectly okay but is different from how your boss would handle it. Your boss will then say the most ominous words in the world: "Could you drop by my office?" She may be a yeller and a screamer and thus you're about to have your day ruined (see Chapter 12 on looking for another job). Or she may be the rational type who will sanely bring the problem to your attention and discuss the need to fix it or prevent it in the future.

Though the latter approach is, of course, preferable, a good girl hates criticism no matter how it's delivered. That's because, like so many things, she takes it personally. The criticism is not simply about her work, but about her. ("If I were really good, I wouldn't have screwed up.") If the criticism comes from a boss whom she feels very connected to, it's a double whammy. ("If she likes me, how can she say that?")

When you take criticism this personally, it's likely to trigger a defensive reaction. You may get sullen, prickly, tearful, or argumentative.

This kind of defensive reaction causes two big problems. Often, the more strongly you resist criticism, the more aggressive your criticizer becomes. The boss ends up saying something stronger and sharper to drive her point home better—and that's likely to leave you feeling even worse.

There's a long-term repercussion as well. According to Pepper Schwartz, professor of sociology at the University of Washington, studies show that bosses avoid giving criticism to women who take it too personally. "Rather than face your reaction," she said, "they decide over time not to say anything. But then you don't hear what you need to hear. It's through criticism that you grow and learn and improve."

When I was in my twenties my boss told me I dug in my heels too much when he offered criticism. It won't surprise you to learn that the first reaction I had in mind was, "No, I don't!" But a little voice whispered that if I knew what was good for me, I'd stand there and nod my head in agreement. Over time, I've learned two techniques for responding to criticism.

The first I picked up from one of the gutsiest girls I've ever worked with. When her boss criticized her she would listen carefully and then she would play back exactly what her boss had just said. She'd say something like, "Steve, it sounds that you're very concerned that I haven't been such-and-such. I can see how you might have thought that." At first this tactic struck me as not only nervy, but dangerous. Why draw even more attention to the criticism by repeating it? It might add to the legitimacy of the boss's complaint by making it appear that you were pleading guilty.

But that's not what happens. When you repeat back what your boss has said, you immediately dissolve the tension in the room because you've given your boss credit for her perceptions. As a boss I'm always expecting an employee to get defensive about criticism, and it's a relief when she seems open to what I have to say. Believe it or not, it also takes the sting out of the criticism once you've articulated it yourself. It's a little bit like lancing a boil.

Your next move is to offer a solution. Ideally your boss will have a few suggestions, but many bosses just aren't good at that. They're so relieved to get their gripe off their chest that they'll just let it lie there on the desk in front of you like an ugly slab of raw meat. It may be up to you to offer a game plan. This, too, helps take the sting away because you've moved on to a more positive course. Spell out what you might do to improve and put it in steps, if possible—with a timetable.

If you're feeling upset or ready to burst into tears, tell your boss that you have some thoughts about improving, but you want to think about them with a clear head and you'll get back to her. There's been so much written on why women shouldn't cry at work, but what those articles generally fail to take into account is that crying is often a reflexive reaction you can't easily control. I've never been a crier, but friends of mine have told me that they've felt their eyes tear up when they least expected it and there's almost no way to stop. That's why the best approach is to leave (leave, not flee) the scene and come back later when you're feeling less emotional.

What if the criticism isn't warranted? I think you still have to acknowledge the perception. ("I can see how you would have drawn this conclusion. . . .") Then offer a game plan on correcting that perception.

# WHY YOU MUST STOP BEING A "BARNEY BOSS"

Playing the pleaser role at work doesn't just involve your boss. It's also about wanting to please the people who work for you.

I don't think I'm stepping out of line here to say that many women feel a nurturing side of their personality take over when they finally have people reporting to them. Whether it's twenty-two-year-olds just out of college or women in their thirties struggling with what they want to do with their lives or fifty-year-olds facing a midlife crisis, I feel an urge to help them, guide them, yes, I admit it, even mother them a little. I once had a smart young woman working for me who was in the throes of a painful divorce and she told me that a pivotal moment for her had been a dream she'd had that involved me. I was driving a car, with her as a passenger in the front seat and her husband in the back. The back of the car had suddenly broken off and I had driven away with just her, leaving the husband (a real bozo, incidentally) lying in the street. She felt the dream had told her that everything would be okay, that I'd take care of her. I have to say that when someone tells me something like that, I go to bed with a warm, fuzzy feeling.

Taking a mother hen or earth mother approach to being a boss suits the good girl just fine. She gets to be in charge, but she gets to be nice, too. She may run an area or department in which everyone has a voice, nobody gets scolded, and all the cards are on the table. She wants her subordinates to think of her as the best boss they've ever had.

You *could* call it the *Barney and Our Gang* approach to being a boss: "I love you, you love me, we're a happy family."

To be perfectly candid, when I was first a boss I chose a Barney style, not simply because I felt comfortable with it, but because I thought it would get me results. The nicer I was to my employees, the better they would perform, I assumed—and the more loyalty I would engender.

Does the Barney approach work? There's been a lot written lately on the value of women's nurturing style of leadership. But I've come to believe that, though you don't want to be known as the Queen of Mean, the Barney style doesn't work either. Watching Barney gives you one of those terrible lows you feel after eating too much sugar, and playing Barney the boss will do the same to your staff.

All I have to do is think of the most dynamic, exciting bosses I've had. Yes, they were nice, but they were never overly nice. Yes, they were fair, but out of the blue they could seem perfectly arbitrary. At times they were moody, unpredictable, leaving one wondering what they really had on their minds. Though they offered compliments, they were select in their praise. They had favorites and they fostered competitiveness. And they never once tried to be my best friend.

My philosophy has been influenced not just by my experience with bosses, but also by what I've learned from being one. What I've come to see after fifteen years of having people report to me is that the earth mother tends to produce a certain type of worker: slugs. If you are too nice or too generous or too lenient, your employees will gradually stretch the rules because they know they can get away with it. They arrive late, leave early, make personal calls, eat lots of messy snacks at their desks, chat with friends, disappear for what seems like hours, and hang posters of Fabio at their work stations. They may also gradually lower their work standards, figuring that if you didn't say anything the first time you won't now. Like children, they keep pushing to see how far they can go.

Messy desks and Fabio pictures aren't the only problems. If you're an earth mother to your charges, they will soon be finding ways for you to take care of more and more of their needs. They will take up your time talking endlessly about their dilemmas (personal as well as business). They will ask you to solve their problems, and hand in work that you must finish or fine-tune.

A good girl worries that if she isn't real nice, she'll be viewed as too tough, mean, perhaps even bitchy. Someone once said that a guy earns a description as ruthless for bombing a small country; a woman earns it for not returning a phone call.

And yet people crave a certain "bossiness" from their bosses, even female ones. Without it there's a lack of excitement and momentum, no healthy sense of reward and repercussion. "The truth is," says sociologist Pepper Schwartz, "people want to be directed. It relaxes them to know that someone is leading them. Without that authority, you make people nervous."

Be thoughtful, but don't be a pushover. Be fair, but ultimately do what *you* want, based on what you think is best. A few other pointers:

1. Create house rules. Employees actually like having rules. I don't mean hard-ass, obnoxious rules but sensible basics about expense accounts, vacations, protocol. You should periodically send out refresher memos or changes in the status quo. These memos are not only titillating because everyone analyzes them, but they also convey a sense of order.
2. Don't always aim for consensus. Linguist Deborah Tannen, Ph.D., author of *You Just Don't Understand* and *Talking 9–5*, says that men are driven by a need to achieve and maintain the upper hand, while women seek to confirm and support—and to reach consensus. That's certainly the good-girl way. You strive for consensus among those who work for you so that everyone will feel happy, "empowered," and committed.

And yet any bold, gutsy idea is bound to have dissenters. If you try to make everybody happy, you will end up diluting the idea or throwing it out.

Nothing has taught me more about the danger of consensus than creating magazine covers. You soon learn that some of the best-selling covers are those that people scrunch up their noses over. One of my most successful covers at *Child* was a shot of a little boy I discovered in the lobby of my apartment building. I thought that the picture the art director and I selected captured him looking a little perplexed and tender as he crawled across the floor, but five people I showed it to at the magazine announced, to my complete chagrin, "He looks grouchy." Fortunately, I wasn't influenced by their opinion.

If you've got a great idea backed up by solid research, present it to your staff with confidence and don't look to them to "approve" it for you. That doesn't mean you want only yes-men and -women working for you. I've had several bosses over the years who didn't want to hear any negatives, and, in the long run, they suffered because they got no feedback on the ideas of theirs that didn't work. In the early stages of an idea you always probe to find the possible downside. But once you've made your commitment to a concept, present it to your staff as a fait accompli. There will be people who scrunch up their noses or look miffed; simply thank them for their input and move on. Psychologist Judith Jordan says that ultimately these people may like you more despite their initial protests: "If you show respect for their opinion, but acknowledge that your instincts are taking you in a different direction, you model something very important for them—that you trust your gut and go with it."

3. Foster a little competition. Though employees want you to be fair, they also thrive when there's healthy competition. Send out a memo praising a particular employee's accomplishment. Give the person with the great idea a chance to present it elsewhere in the company.

4. Sound firm. Say "Please get it to me 9:00 A.M. Monday" rather than "It would be great if you could get it to me Monday."

5. Run Gutsy Meetings. Employers give the impression they enjoy easygoing meetings where they get to shoot the breeze, laugh and joke. But what they really want from you are tight, short meetings with clear agendas and resolutions. Only invite those who are absolutely necessary. Distribute a written agenda of the general points you want addressed. Don't allow interruptions or distractions. Keep it to half an hour if possible, an hour tops, and end by summarizing the key decisions and the steps to be taken (along with deadlines about when people will get back).

# BUT NONE OF THIS MEANS YOU SHOULD BE A BITCH

When I say that it's important to be tough and firm, by no means do I suggest you be a bitch. There was a time when bitchiness in the corner office had a certain cachet—you got to pretend you were playing a Joan Crawford role in a movie—but those days are over. Though we think of bitches as being tough and mean, I've come to believe that in many cases they are former good girls who are overcompensating. As soon as they feel taken advantage of or threatened, their adrenaline pumps up and they act like Doberman pinschers.

Though bitchiness works short term—people scatter out of your office and immediately begin toeing the line—in the long run it will be your undoing. Employees wait anxiously for bitches to get theirs, do what they can to facilitate that, and gleefully watch as the boom comes down. It's not just a women's issue. Mean bosses of both sexes put themselves in jeopardy these days.

# HOW TO GET PEOPLE TO WORSHIP YOU

I'm about to make a statement that will seem to contradict everything I've said up until now in this chapter. To assure your success, you need to have the people you work with feel a fierce sense of devotion toward you.

How can this make any sense after I've stated you shouldn't worry whether or not people like you. Because liking someone and being devoted to them isn't one and the same thing.

To inspire devotion, you must give people something they secretly want. It doesn't mean you have to be their best friend or mother, bend over backwards for them, do their dirty work, solve their problems, or listen to them describe their herniated disc in great detail. Here's what I think they're really looking for.

# The Secret Thing Your Boss Wants: PASSION

*Your* passion. Yes, your boss expects you to be good at your job, but what she truly wants is for you to be passionate—about what you do, about the department or organization, and yes, passionate about working for her.

Being passionate doesn't mean staying late every night to clean the blackboards. It means demonstrating a turbo-charged enthusiasm for what you're doing *and* what your boss is doing.

An important aspect of showing your passion is what I call "face time." Make your presence known, let your boss in on what's happening, stick your head in her door just to let her see that you're "back," send along thought-provoking articles relating to the business with "Thought you'd be interested" Post-its. In the thick of my good-girl days, I allowed myself to believe that keeping a low profile made my boss happiest because I wasn't being a nudge. But since then I've come to see that absence doesn't make the heart grow fonder.

Management consultant Kathy Strickland, head of the Strickland Group in New York City, who has trained some of my managers, says laughingly that she, too, can't resist this kind of passion. "I often tell the people who work for me that they can feel free to call me with questions or issues, even if it's two in the morning. Generally, they don't. They're good and they solve their own problems. I have this one dynamite person, though, who loves to check in with me, run something by me, and though I know everyone views her as an ass-kisser, I have to admit, I love it."

What you don't want to do is cross the line into making yourself look gushy or needy or desperate for approval. The key is to keep the focus on the work, not yourself.

There are some bosses who just don't like face time, from anyone. What can happen is that the more you try to work your way into the inner circle, the more she'll pull back. "It's not unlike the dance lovers do in which one person is the pursuer and the other the distancer," says psychotherapist Marjorie Lapp. "The harder the pursuer pursues, the more distance the distancer attempts to place between the two of them."

If you keep your antennae up, you'll notice it. Your boss may seem irritated by your having popped into her office or exasperated with some of your questions. She may actually try to create some physical distance, moving back or going behind her desk. The best strategy is to pull back a little and create some room.

# The Secret Thing Your Subordinates Want: PASSION

In this case, their *own* passion. They want to come alive, be in love with what they do, and it takes a certain kind of boss to foster that.

Now, if you were to ask people what kind of boss they like best, they might very well describe a Barney boss—someone who sets up one of those kinder, gentler work environments. Don't believe them. As I said before, the Barney approach not only prevents people from performing at the top of their game, it also, I've come to believe, fails to inspire the fierce adoration you might think it would.

Why not? Consider this scenario: You are about to marry

and you are allowed to determine which kind of marriage it will be:

A. a safe, predictable, fuzzy slipper of a relationship, with okay sex, rated PG

B. an exciting, sometimes unpredictable union with the sexiest sex, rated R

Wouldn't you go for B?

I think it's the same with bosses. Deep down most of us really want a boss who will help us discover our professional G spot, who will find what we're most passionate about and let us run with it, who will give us a sense of our own power and importance. That doesn't happen in a fuzzy slipper of an environment, but rather in a setting that is sometimes pressured and hectic.

The best way to find that G spot?

- Ask individual subordinates how they would do things. Listen not only to their answers, but what it reveals about their thinking, their interests, their desires.
- Charge them up not only about their specific responsibilities but the overall mission. Warren Bennis, author of *Leaders: The Strategies for Taking Charge,* said people yearn to be "part of a worthwhile enterprise."
- Challenge your subordinates to solve their own problems. When they turn to you unrelentingly for advice, tell them you want them to get back to you with possible solutions. They may look wounded initially but solving their own problems will turn them into grown-ups.
- Don't feel you have to be one of them or play down your own powerfulness in the organization. They like it because it rubs off on them.

- Create task forces of several people in your department to generate ideas or solutions.
- Have periodic crunch projects that call for staying late and ordering pizzas.
- Don't reveal *everything*. Keep them curious.
- Ask them to help on special projects and don't feel you have to reward them. In his fabulous book *Hardball: How Politics Is Played Told by One Who Knows the Game,* Christopher Matthews says that "the little secret shared by smart politicians is that people get a kick out of being propositioned. The smart politician knows that in soliciting someone he is not so much making a demand, but offering the person the one thing he himself wants: the opportunity to get involved." A good girl needs to learn this. Give your staff the sense that the best prize is simply being on your team.

## THE SIX MOST IMPORTANT PEOPLE TO CULTIVATE (BESIDES YOUR BOSS)

It's not enough to have a bond with those you work with directly. You must also work constantly to forge alliances with all sorts of people in the organization who may at one point be in a position to help you. These will include people far below your level (mail room, accounts receivable, etc.), people of your rank in other departments, and even major players to whom you don't report directly but whom you may need to consult for information. As a gutsy girl I know says, "You never know when the guys in the print room will be in a position to save your hide."

It's funny that even though women have a knack for forming relationships, they aren't as quick as men are to build these kinds of alliances. "Women have better skills at developing relationships than men, but less understanding of how crucial it is to have them with all sorts of people in the organization," says University of West Florida assistant professor of management Gayle Baugh. "Women take an almost legalistic view of the workplace and feel that informal networks are improper."

In fact, forming these alliances may be more important to your success than having a mentor. It's not that a mentor isn't of great value, but good luck getting one today, or at least getting one who's going to be around tomorrow. In these crazy times you can easily find that your mentor has been lured away by a headhunter, become the victim of a coup, or has finally decided to fulfill her dream of owning her own guest lodge in the Great Smoky Mountains. A gutsy girl knows she can't put all her eggs in one basket. Here are a few of the people you should be forming your alliances with:

- The gatekeepers to power: secretaries. If they like you they will squeeze you into the schedule, keep you posted, even make remarks about your skill that will leave an impression on their boss.
- The keepers of information. In every company there are people in middle or low rank who possess critical information. They are more likely to be forthcoming if they like you. A friend of mine realized recently that someone in her department was leaking valuable information to another company. The man in charge of the company's phone system did a search for her of office telephones that had made calls to that number.
- People who perform basic services that one day you may need urgently. Like the print shop, the mail room, and computer services.
- Cross-departmental employees whose work directly or

indirectly affects yours. When I got to *McCall's* I knew it was critical to get as much information as possible about the reader, and I began to develop a nice relationship with the guy who was in charge of company research. Though some consumer research was done through his office, the magazine was "scored" each month using a questionnaire compiled, mailed, and tabulated by an outside firm many major magazines relied on. Once at a company party I complained to the researcher about how long it took to get the results, and how difficult it was to change the magazine when you didn't know until March how a September issue did. He looked at me with a twinkle and asked, "What if we did it by phone?" He created a whole system that allowed us to get results within three weeks of when the magazine arrived in someone's home.

- Bosses in other departments. You might someday want to work for one of them. Just be careful that you don't develop a buddy-buddiness that threatens your boss.
- Any smart, talented person who once worked with you and is now in another company or business.

How do you get all these various people to form alliances with you? Schmoozing works, so occasionally do boxes of sticky buns and tickets to ball games. But I think the best advice I ever heard on this subject came from Adele Scheele, when she was my career columnist at *Working Woman*: "Ask their opinion of something you're thinking of doing, listen to their answer, and then follow up." More than sticky buns or ball games, people love to have you value their opinion. This works even with those no longer in your company. Pick up the phone from time to time and ask their advice.

# Strategy #5: A Gutsy Girl Walks and Talks Like a Winner

This is a chapter about style versus substance. Though perhaps I should rephrase that just a little. This is a chapter about style *and* substance.

Okay, I know you're feeling tempted to skip over this section, but please don't. To a good girl, style is a frivolous word, even a dirty word, because it's the antithesis of the ethic she works by. A good girl believes that success should be based on the quality of her work, not on how good she looks or sounds. When she sees rewards handed to someone who simply talks a good game (or worse, simply looks the part), she's appalled. She may conclude that the person making the decision has his values out of whack—or perhaps he is simply overwhelmed by a throbbing in his groin. A good-girl friend of mine complained to me the other day that a very flashy woman in her company had just gotten a VP title, which has always eluded my friend. "It's not fair," she said. "I've paid my dues and she hasn't. They ought to call her vice president of pizzazz."

The truth is that paying your dues in the form of accomplishing certain goals doesn't necessarily get you into the club you want to belong to. You have to look and sound like you deserve to be a member. The reason I didn't say you *also* have to look and sound the part is that in some cases looking and sounding alone are enough, as much as it might gall us to realize that. I once briefly had a woman on my staff who didn't have enough skill to edit a menu, but she went on to land one great job after another. This drove the people who worked under her nutty because to them she had such a shortage of real talent. Yet she speaks with utter assurance and dynamism, dresses beautifully, and when you are in her presence you're convinced she is a megastar.

Will her lack of substance catch up with her? Maybe. But maybe not. What you have to do is stop being annoyed by women like her and focus on the more positive aspect of the image issue. Though style alone can sell you, combining it with substance gives you the double whammy. If you're talented at what you do and mix it with a sizable flash factor, you are almost guaranteed success.

What it really comes down to is taking the idea of gutsiness and translating it to the way you look, sound, and come across. And at times that will mean doing something differently from the way you've always been told.

# WHY TALENT AND BRILLIANCE AREN'T ENOUGH

Even as you accept the need to be gutsy with your image, it may still bug you that it has to be this way. You'd think that in a world of grown-ups, performance alone would matter. In our culture, however, we grow up learning that packaging carries lots of weight, and we soon transfer this lesson to judging people.

It's not always a matter of values gone askew. Sometimes those doing the judging simply don't have enough information to access your level of ability so they judge how deep it *seems* to be, based on your presentation of yourself.

I remember the exact moment I learned this terrible truth. I was just twenty-two and had been an editorial assistant in *Glamour's* merchandising department for a couple of months when suddenly the place was abuzz over a new assistant who would soon be joining the department. The editors who'd interviewed her were raving about how dynamic she was and they kept adding the phrase, "Wait till you see her portfolio." When I'd first gotten out of college, several people advised me to put together a portfolio, but I hadn't bothered because it seemed so presumptuous. At that point all I had to show were articles I'd written for my college magazine, and I couldn't imagine that people would be wowed by pieces like "My Search for the Ghost of Union College."

But the new editorial assistant, Debbie, hadn't felt the least bit reserved about showing off what she had done. As soon as she started I made it my business to get a glimpse at the famed portfolio and my jaw actually dropped as I went through it. The portfolio itself was professional quality (genuine leather), but the stuff in it was totally idiotic. She had one photographic series she'd titled "Ten Little Indians," which consisted of ten pictures of her holding up from one to ten of her fingers. The only conclusion I could draw was that she had hypnotized the editors before they looked at it. What she had actually done was dazzle them with her self-assurance and gumption.

From that day on I understood that things like full-grain leather could compensate for a lot. What has continued to surprise me, however, is how much flash matters, even when you have plenty of skill and experience.

When I was called by a headhunter about the job of editor-in-chief of *Child*, I felt an incredible rush, not only because it sounded like a dream job, but also because I believed that with my background, I'd have a real shot at it. I'd been generating ideas and editing articles about being a woman and being a mother for years. Over breakfast with the headhunter, I realized after the first ten minutes that it would be pointless to go into lots of details about the columns I'd started or the ideas I'd generated. He was a smart guy, but he had never worked at a magazine. Of course, the fact that I'd been editing relevant material for a long time carried weight—that's how I'd gotten in the door—but there was certainly no way he could have looked at a section I'd taken over in a magazine and have made an assessment of my contribution.

My next meeting was scheduled with two people on the business side of the company and I realized that they might be no better equipped to judge my skills. How was I going to stand out?

I considered drumming up a presentation with slides or poster board. But I imagined their eyes glazing over as I described my special knack for creating article "sidebars." Then I did something that surprised the hell out of me. I called a friend and asked to borrow her black silk Calvin Klein suit and I made an appointment to have my hair blown dry and styled before the second interview. If people weren't going to pay close attention to my background, perhaps they would pay attention to how I looked and sounded.

To this day I'm convinced I owe part of my success to an Infiniti 2000 blow-dryer.

Don't let any of this discourage you. As you learn to be gutsier with your image, you will find that it's not only fun but very empowering. Looking and sounding like a winner makes you feel like one.

# HOW TO SEE YOURSELF LIKE EVERYONE ELSE DOES

Before you can begin to tinker with your style, you need to get a sense of how you actually come across to people—and that can be a very tricky thing to do. Quite often, especially when we're in the early stages of our work life, how we perceive ourselves doesn't bear much resemblance to how others view us.

I call this the Dr. Kildare Syndrome. When I was thirteen and used to walk up and down the streets of Glens Falls, New York, in my Dr. Kildare shirt, I truly believed that people thought I was a doctor. That same kind of perception gap exists for many of us. What you consider candidness may come across to others as poor judgment. What you think of as terrific exuberance may be viewed by others as immaturity. Since it's so hard to see yourself, how do you begin to determine the perception others have of you? There are a couple of ways.

## Pay attention to the five-second comments people make to you about yourself

It would be nice if we could count on our bosses and co-workers to offer beneficial observations and advice about our behavior, but unfortunately that rarely happens. They do, however, manage to let their impressions sneak out in little ways that we generally ignore or mistake for either humor or grouchiness. When someone teases you about dressing "down" or keeping a low profile in a meeting or skipping out early on an important company party, you need to pay attention to the underlying message. Yes, it could be just a cheap shot, but it could also accurately signal that you're dressing wrong for the job, hiding your light under a bushel, or failing to schmooze enough with those who matter.

# Watch a videotape of yourself

Okay, this sounds a little far-fetched. But today so many work events are videotaped that it may be easy to get hold of a tape that features you making a presentation or just being a participant, and you'll find that this is the best possible wake-up call about how you come across.

Trust me, it can be a shock to see for the first time how you handle yourself in a work setting. In my own case I felt like I needed CPR after viewing myself on tape. I had a way of flapping my arms around when I talked that made me look like a pterodactyl. But once you get over the initial shock, you can evaluate what's working and what's not. Ask yourself these questions:

- How's my energy level?
- How's my posture?
- What do my gestures and body language convey?
- Do I seem to be connecting with people?
- Is my voice forceful and effective?
- Are people paying attention to me as I speak?
- Do people in authority address their comments to me?

# Answer this question: Does your boss's boss know who you are?

If you're not known among those in power positions on the next level (or levels) of your company, you're not doing enough to network and/or highlight your accomplishments.

# Answer this question: How often does your boss trot you out to showcase your skills to higher management or your industry?

From time to time your boss will have the opportunity to show off star employees—for instance, by having them speak at conventions or industry functions, by having them make presentations of their research to higher-ups. As a boss I can tell you that the employees I choose to do this are those who I know will make *me* look good. But it's not simply a matter of their being highly skilled in their jobs. They also have to come across as dynamos. If they don't look "right," I'm nervous about putting them out in front because of how people will perceive them. If you see others being shown off and you're not, it's time to consider your image.

# THE HOLLYWOOD STARLET TRICK EVEN YOU CAN USE

President John Kennedy said that energy was everything, and if there were only one packaging tip I could give to the good girls who have worked for me, it would be, "Get some zip."

The right clothes and the right body language won't make up for operating on only four cylinders.

If your energy is consistently on the low side, you need to take a look at your lifestyle. Studies show that the four biggest energy zappers are lack of sleep, stress, poor eating, and lack of exercise. Stress is misleading because we've developed a false sense that it actually charges us up. It does momentarily, but according to Margaret Chesney, an epidemiologist at the University of California School of Medicine in San Francisco, if the pressure continues, it begins to erode both our energy and our resistance to illness.

My energy level has always been pretty high, sustained by megadoses of caffeine. But even still, I find there are times when I'm about to go into a meeting or make a presentation when I'm feeling about as exciting as a bowl of overcooked pasta. In those cases I've learned to try to do a few things to jump-start myself, sometimes simply walking around for a few minutes beforehand. Sitting up in my chair also seems to help. When I was at *Mademoiselle*, we did this fun little article once on how the stars stay beautiful, and it was filled with silly stuff like taping one's breasts with gaffer's tape to give them the look of ripe cantaloupes. But one tip actually sounded worthwhile. Before they have publicity shots done, some actresses reportedly jump up and down and vigorously huff and puff just to make themselves look full of vitality for the photo. I haven't been forced to use this technique yet but I keep it in reserve.

# THE NEW (AND IMPROVED) RULES OF DRESS FOR SUCCESS

Do you remember *Dress for Success* by John Molloy? If you've been in the workforce less than twelve years, you might not be familiar with it but you may have felt its effect indirectly. Mr. Molloy's book was primarily a guide for men, but he threw in tips for women that profoundly influenced how the majority of working women showed up at the office for many years afterwards. Here's the kind of advice he was offering:

There is one firm and dramatic step women can take toward professional equality with men. They can adopt a business uniform. Beyond any doubt the uniform should be a skirted suit and blouse. In most cases the suit should be dark and the blouse should contrast. It should not be pinched at the waist to exaggerate the bust. Colors avoided should be bright red, bright orange, and bright anything else.

Mr. Molloy also said in his book that the dress is the "ultimate seduction garment."

It was in response to such gospel that millions of women like me donned dark, man-tailored suits, white shirts, and floppy bow ties that not only made us all look alike but resulted in our never being able to walk down the aisle of an airplane without being asked for a pillow or an extra bottle of Mr and Mrs T Bloody Mary mix.

Molloy didn't intend anything malicious. He was just trying to help women by putting us in uniforms that he believed would make it easier for men to accept our presence in the office.

The trouble is that Molloy played into the good-girl part of our nature by telling us that if we didn't follow the rules, we would fail or at the very least be called a slut. Times, of course, have changed. The floppy bow tie has gone the way of the poor boy sweater and Mr. Molloy has deleted the above advice from his book. Yet many of us still err on the side of caution when we dress because those old words are in the back of our heads.

Confusing matters even more is the fact that there are no contemporary guidelines around to replace what Molloy said. There are only two things we can be reasonably sure of today:

1. Different companies, different industries, and different parts of the country vary significantly in their dress codes. Those codes are often unwritten and not always clear.
2. If you wear a red blazer to an industry conference, it's a safe bet to say that at least 60 percent of the other women in the room will have one on, too.

Though there are no hard-and-fast rules these days, these are the basic guidelines I believe a gutsy girl should dress by:

- Always, always dress as if you were in the job you aspire to. This advice has been spoken many times before, but good girls don't always adhere to it. They fear that they'll seem too presumptuous dressing "powerfully." Don't worry if a few of your co-workers give you a who-does-she-think-she-is? look when you walk in wearing a $400 suit that you spent your last dime on. The people making the decisions will be impressed.
- If you're not good at dressing yourself, turn yourself over to someone who can do it for you. One option, of course, is to use the personal shopper at a department store—though buyer beware: many of them tend to go overboard. I tried the personal shopper route and I ended up posing for several weeks as a sixty-five-year-old matron from Greenwich, Connecticut. What finally worked for me was to find a couple of designers whose

clothes always looked great on me and I never buy anything else.

- Be gutsy enough to pack away the red blazers. Just as the navy suit and floppy tie formed a business uniform in the late seventies, the bold red or color-blocked jacket took its place in the fast-paced eighties. That kind of look may have gotten women noticed at one point, but now it's almost as much a uniform as the old one. And the accessories that get piled on with this look—pins, scarves, bracelets—can make you appear like an overdecorated room in a designer show house.

   Kendall Farr, who was my fashion editor at *Working Woman*, says that a far classier and more distinctive look is one of understated elegance. It starts with a simple but perfectly cut solid-colored suit in a fine fabric, and all that gets added is perhaps a great watch and a pair of antique earrings. Think of Mary Steenburgen in *Philadelphia*. It takes nerve to go the pared-down route because at first you feel underdressed. But it will give you a powerful presence.

- Wear the clothes and accessories with the maximum style you can get away with in your company and field. You probably have a decent sense of what's considered appropriate for your firm, your industry, and your region of the United States. What works in New York can bomb in Dallas. The outfit that will dazzle them in advertising will get you banished in banking. I'm not going to advise that you be in the vanguard of breaking down existing dress codes in your company—it's really essential to stay within the parameters. But I think you should go absolutely as far as those parameters allow, rather than stay safely in the middle. Dressing with as much gutsiness as you can get away with will add energy to your image and make people notice and remember you.

I ran this theory by a woman who teaches management courses and she hinted that I was out of my mind. She said that a woman must dress conservatively and not do anything to stand out as different from "them."

And yet, every place I turn, the women with clout have abandoned any kind of uniform. Linda Fairstein, the head of the New York County sex-crimes prosecution unit, has said that she believes her feminine suits by Escada and Calvin Klein give her more authority than "dumpy but sincere lady-lawyer suits."

- When in doubt, or when you need to look authoritative, do not wear pants.
- If you need clout, wear high heels.
- Never wear stockings that give your legs a fake suntan.
- Wear makeup—and always freshen it after lunch.

# WHAT YOUR BODY SAYS ABOUT YOU

A very successful entrepreneur told me that several months after she had started her consulting business, a client asked if he could videotape one of their sessions for reference. She agreed and then a few days later borrowed the tape because she'd begun to get curious about how she came across. What she saw horrified her.

"Through at least half the session, I was covering my mouth with my hand," she recalls. "It was if I was saying, 'I'm new at this and I don't have much faith in what I'm saying.'"

After body language was introduced as a hot topic in the 1970s, there followed dozens of books and articles on the subject, some of which I wrote myself because editors were always looking for pieces on the subject. Today it's not as hot and sexy a topic, and yet body language remains a powerful communicator of your feelings about yourself and how you're reacting to a specific situation.

Good girls especially have to be on guard about their body language. If you feel uncertain or insecure, it will show up in your posture, your gestures, your facial expressions. When I was in my twenties I felt like my body was a walking advertisement for the self-doubt I experienced in certain professional situations. One of my most hilarious memories involves going to a press event for Paul Newman's new salad dressing. I was sitting at a table, wolfing down the free hors d'oeuvres (something poor single girls always do in New York), when the press agent unexpectedly brought Newman over for me to meet. I jumped up in such an awkward manner that the strap of my purse, which was draped over my shoulder, became tangled around the chair, and once I was on my feet, the chair was actually dangling from my neck, like the world's largest pendant. "Please sit down," Newman said curtly, looking at me as if I were a total doofus.

Even after you've developed a comfort level with your body in work situations, residual insecurities can sneak out in your gestures and movements. Once, during a rehearsal for a speech that I was dreading, I noticed in the mirror that I was literally wringing my hands as I talked. There's lots of fascinating information on body language, but these are the two most important points for good girls:

1. Be the boss of your body language. So much of the time body language is *reactive*. Your boss criticizes a tactic you take and your shoulders slump. A boisterous male colleague monopolizes a meeting and you start sinking into your seat. A client you're meeting with seems bored with what you're saying and you start playing with your hair. Develop an awareness of your body language: Is it in overdrive (you're using lots of hand signals and imagi-

nary quotation marks)? Has it turned wimpy? Once you're more aware of it, you can modify it. Nancy Austin once told me she noticed over time that whenever she used one finger to point during a presentation, the men in the room became uncomfortable. She experimented and found that they didn't seem threatened if she pointed with two fingers.

2. Dare to hold someone's gaze. In his classic book *Body Language*, Julius Fast said that of all parts of the human body that are used to transmit information, the eyes are the most important and can convey the most subtle nuances. And the most important technique of what he called eye management is the look or the stare. I learned the power of holding someone's gaze in a fabulous experiment. When I was a writer at *Glamour*, I was often given wacky assignments, like spending a night at a sex-toy party or seeing if I could meet a man at a health club (I refused to do "My Week at a Nudist Camp"). One of the most fascinating assignments was writing a piece about "eye power" because part of the research involved keeping a "staring diary" for two weeks. I had to stare at friends, colleagues, men on the subway, men in bars, even men coming out of porno movie houses, all in an attempt to see how people reacted. I learned from my research with Dr. Alan Mazur, Ph.D., a professor of sociology at Syracuse University, that staring rituals are part of our biological makeup and there are several rules about staring that we unconsciously obey (just the way baboons do).

For instance, in a conversation between two people, the listener always feels an obligation to look at the speaker but the speaker often glances away as he or she talks, so as not to make the listener uncomfortable. One exception: The listener is less likely to maintain a steady gaze at the speaker if he has substantially more power.

When a man and a woman meet or encounter each other, says Mazur, women are much more apt to be the first to avert their eyes because it's an instinctive way we display submissiveness. As part of my assignment I had to resist the good-girl urge to look away first. Instead, I would hold a person's gaze until he broke eye contact. What I learned from all this startled me. Maintaining eye contact didn't make me uncomfortable, as I had expected it might. Rather it made me feel powerful, in control—and people seemed mesmerized.

Try this experiment for a day or two. As you greet people at work, pass them in the hallway, or talk to them at meetings, watch yourself and note how much of the time you are the first to avert your eyes. Then begin to change that pattern. When you shake someone's hand, hold their gaze as long as possible, allowing them to avert their eyes first. If you're about to speak at a meeting, let your eyes sweep around the table and briefly hold the gaze of each person. You'll discover that holding someone's gaze not only gives you a sense of power, but it also forges a stronger connection.

One of the things that struck me about Ivana Trump when she came to lunch at *McCall's* after writing a piece for us was how strongly she held my gaze during lunch. She seemed to really *relate* to me. I laughed when, later, someone on my staff who sat at the *other* end of the table told me, "I felt like Ivana really connected with me. She looked at me through the entire lunch."

One caution about staring: be careful with your boss. Think of him as the dominant baboon in the colony and never attempt to stare him down.

# HOW TO ENTER A ROOM AS IF YOU OWN IT

Whether you're walking into a conference room with ten people already seated or walking onto a stage to take part in a panel, it's hard not to feel awkward—and also hard to keep that awkwardness fully contained. When Liz Smith, gutsy girl par excellence, was a contributing editor of *McCall's*, I was struck by how fabulous she looked every time she entered a room. She was always the essence of poise and power. Several times she came to company cocktail parties and you would have thought a movie star had just arrived by the way people gawked at her entrance. I kept wondering what it was about her. Certainly her clothes played a big part. She wears these beautiful signature blazers—for day or night. Also, I think she's one of those people who come out of the womb with an aura around them. But I finally realized that there's something else that makes her seem so in control. She never, ever touches her hands to her face the way so many women do, particularly when they walk into a new or stressful setting. Studies show that women tend to engage in far more "self-related" activity than men, such as touching their face or pushing back their hair. When you touch your hand to your face or hair, you're announcing to the room that you're worried about how you look and how you'll come across, and everyone picks up subliminally on that insecurity.

## THE MYTH OF TALKING TOUGH

Just as women were encouraged to dress like men in the 70s and 80s, we were also told we ought to talk like them too. In his 1977 bestseller *Success*, author Michael Korda said that "hitting hard" was the first rule for success for women and he issued this strong advisory: "Ambitious women must learn that they can't win by charm, persuasion and tactful pressure."

Korda said women should try to sound even tougher than men. "Suggest radical innovations," he said, "talk tough, accuse other people of timidity and 'good guy' behavior . . . take the hard line on every occasion. If a man suggests that the situation calls for a stiff letter, say 'stiff letter, hell, let's sue.'" Korda and many other experts suggested that women completely play down their femininity when they spoke. They shouldn't talk about their feelings or personal experiences, or, God forbid, sound too sensitive.

There are several major drawbacks to this talk-like-a-man approach. As communications consultant Pam Zarit says, it's the equivalent of wearing a tight helmet on your head all day long.

And, as many women began to discover, this advice wasn't necessarily *right*—at least in many instances. Charm works, persuasion works, and so does tactful pressure. And more and more, the feminine perspective is perceived as extremely valuable.

When you let yourself speak naturally, it's both exhilarating and effective. My own liberation came through some work I did with Zarit.

I'd actually begun taking public speaking lessons after a disastrous presentation I made at *Glamour*. While an assistant in the merchandising department, I was asked to cover for a sick editor and give a short talk to store buyers on fashion trends for fall. Someone on staff who critiqued my presentation said I had come across like "a funeral director discussing coffin options." It wasn't until I hooked up with Zarit, however, that I feel I hit my stride. The first thing she did was encourage me to talk from abbreviated notes rather than a prepared speech and to use lots of anecdotes, because she felt

I sounded best when I was talking conversationally. In fact, she said, the executives she worked with who were the most charismatic speakers were those who didn't try to keep the unique aspects of their personalities under wrap for fear that they wouldn't conform to some professional model.

I soon found that this made me feel far more comfortable—and effective—as a public speaker. But something else happened, too. I began to use the same approach in one-on-one dealings. Instead of going by a script, saying what I thought a person in my position ought to say or what I assumed the other person wanted to hear, I became more and more comfortable saying what was on my mind.

Don't be afraid of the sound of your own voice. Growing up, girls of my generation heard that they should let the boy do the talking. We were supposed to ask lots of questions, nod enthusiastically, and punctuate their soliloquies with comments like "Oh wow."

That kind of instruction seems to haunt us in our careers, no matter how much of value we have to say. In her best-selling book *You Just Don't Understand*, linguist Deborah Tannen cites research on how women with expertise in a certain field showed support for their male conversational partners (saying things like "Yeah" and "That's right") far more than the nonexpert they were talking to showed support for *them*. The women not only didn't wield their expertise as power, but tried to play it down and make up for it through extra assenting behavior. They acted as if their expertise were something to *hide*. The need to be nice and develop rapport subjugated any desire to show off knowledge and experience.

Tannen believes that one of the reasons men get into lecturing women is *because* women listen attentively and don't interrupt with challenges, sidetracks, or "matching." Men also attempt to lecture other men, but the male listeners are experienced at butting in with their own opinions.

Though women may think they're doing the right thing by being such attentive listeners, Tannen wonders if men may actually be disappointed in a conversational partner who turns out to have nothing to say.

Show off your expertise, offer your insight. You'll be surprised at how much they like it. And don't be embarrassed about your experience as a female. When *McCall's* hosted a roundtable discussion with the seven female U.S. senators, Senator Barbara Boxer of California said, "One thing I sense we do more than our male colleagues is use our experiences. We don't put our experiences over here and our senatorship over there. It becomes one."

Senator Patty Murray of Washington concurred: "We bring our personal struggles to the Senate—and we're not afraid to talk about them and fight for them. That's why you're seeing the women senators coalescing around budget, health, education and workplace issues—because we struggle with these at home."

# THREE LITTLE WAYS TO SOUND GUTSIER

Though you shouldn't be afraid to sound like a woman, you don't want to sound like a good girl.

## I. Always Cut to the Chase

When it's time to pitch an idea to me, good-girl editors often start off giving lots of background information, and slowly wind their way to what the essence of the story is going to be. By the time they get there, I'm in a stupor or convinced that the idea isn't good because if it was the editor would be bursting at the seams.

The gutsy girls, on the other hand, start with a clear, powerful working title that snares you immediately. Then they succinctly build their case. I had an editor pitch an idea the other day with the title "Love Map to Your Husband's Body: His 7 Best Pleasure Points." I can't help it—I wanna know more.

You should use the same get-to-the-point strategy when you talk in business. And come to think of it, the catchy title idea could work well, too. Consider what a great reaction you'd get if you announced to your boss that you had "A Surprising New Way to Boost Sales," "Software that Will Revolutionize How the Department Does Business," or "Four Steps that Will Trim the Fat off the Budget."

These cut-to-the-chase guidelines ought to be used in every memo you write, too.

# 2. Never Start a Statement with "I Don't Know"

Carol Gilligan found that the girls she studied often used that phrase to introduce their most astute observations, and I've noticed how often women use it too, even when they are about to offer a legitimate opinion.

# 3. Don't Hedge

Years ago, long before I heard of Deborah Tannen, I interviewed a linguist named Robin Lakoff, who had documented the speech patterns of women. According to Lakoff, throughout history women have listened more than they've spoken and agreed more than they have confronted. They have been delicate and indirect when they've spoken, and have said dangerous things in such a way that their impact would be felt after the speaker was out of range of the hearer's retaliation. They have had to do this in order to survive and even flourish without control over economic, physical, or social reality.

Though the same conditions don't exist, many of the speaking patterns remain, and they can undermine you in a business setting. They make you sound as if you're confused, unsure, or uncommitted. In your language you want to watch out for words that convey impreciseness, such as *so* and *such*, hedges like *kind of*, intonation patterns that make statements resemble questions, and excruciating politeness.

# A FEW CANDID WORDS ABOUT HONESTY

While we're on the subject of talking, I'd like to say a few words about telling the truth.

Good girls learn very early that honesty is the best policy, and that principle will serve you well in your work. Beyond the morality issue, if you become known as untrustworthy, it will stymie many of your efforts. But on the other hand—how do I say this without having you think I'm a terrible person—there's such a thing as being too honest for your own good. Let me put that another way. It's important to tell the truth but you don't always have to tell the whole truth.

A good girl has a tendency to go overboard in her truth telling, offering up gory details that aren't required and could end up hurting her. Several months ago, for instance, I received a letter from two women, in business together, who wanted to talk to me about a line extension idea for the magazine. Intrigued, I invited them in for a meeting. One of the first questions I asked was how they came to start their own company, and they took turns talking about the work experience they had before they met. Each volunteered that she had been "let go" from a large corporation due to downsizing. Now, there's nothing wrong with that—lots of us get fired and lots of terrific entrepreneurial ventures are born that way. But "I was let go" is a loaded sentence, one capable of leaving even the most open-minded among us seeing a large FIRED sign above the person's head during the entire conversation. In certain instances these women might need to be forthcoming, *but it wasn't necessary in this case*. Each could have simply said, "I worked for so-and-so and then decided to go into business for myself," which is exactly what a man would have said.

Resist the good-girl urge to confess when no one would expect you to anyway. And if it *is* essential for you to reveal something negative, remember that there's more than one way to tell the truth. The best lesson I ever learned about this is from Merrie Spaeth, president of Spaeth Communications, Inc., in Dallas and former media adviser to President Reagan. "When you speak, it doesn't matter to your listener whether you use a good word—one that reflects well on you—or a bad one," she says. "However, if you give the listener a choice between good words and bad words, he is virtually *certain* to remember the bad ones."

So instead of bad words like *trouble, fail, disaster*, and *incomplete*, use lots of good ones, like *solution, fix, turnaround*, and *progress*.

# HOW A GUTSY GIRL TAKES A COMPLIMENT

Quite simply, she takes it. A good girl, on the other hand, always pooh-poohs compliments. You tell her she looks terrific and she says, "Oh, I don't. This suit is ancient." You say she did a great job and she replies, "Well I wish I'd had more time." She's afraid that if she accepts the compliment without question or qualification, she'll appear egotistical.

A few months ago I was seated at the same table as Sen. Carol Moseley Braun of Illinois at a luncheon in her honor. Midway through the meal she was asked to speak for a few moments about programs and legislation she was focusing on. What a speaker she was—eloquent, forceful, charming. Later over dessert she happened to mention that she was reading a book about oratory, and this overbearing guy at the table announced, "You're a fantastic speaker, you don't need to do one single thing differently." Perhaps due to my residual good-girl tendencies, I sat there waiting for the senator to demur, to say something like, "Well, there's always room for improvement." Instead she offered a big smile and said, "Thank you very much." It was incredibly refreshing and effective.

# A GUTSY GIRL'S SECRET WEAPON

One of the best parts of winning *Glamour* magazine's college contest was the prize trip to New York and Great Britain. In New York we stayed at the old Biltmore Hotel, where we were pampered like crazy and got a taste of life as we'd never known it. On one of our mornings in New York several of us had been sent to a hotel suite to have our hair done by one of the top hairdressers in New York, in preparation for a photo shoot. Room-service breakfast was running about twenty minutes late, and finally the fashion stylist on *Glamour*'s staff, this fabulously self-assured blonde, picked up the phone, dialed the room-service number, and in a chilly voice announced that if we didn't have breakfast immediately, there would be serious consequences.

The hairdresser looked at me and said gleefully, "Doesn't she sound just like the Duchess of Windsor?"

From that day forward I decided that was how *I* wanted to sound. Over the years I did learn to use the Duchess of Windsor tone on more than a few airline sales agents and a few people whom I dealt with professionally.

But you know what? It never really worked for me. I not only felt uncomfortable trying to be overly tough or nasty, but it was also never very effective.

Since then I have discovered a much better approach: graciousness. You are polite, charming, eager to be understanding.

The woman who is the master at this is Ivana. I expected her to be snooty, not based on anything I'd read, but rather on the sheer fact that she'd been so pampered for years—and also because so many of the celebrities we interview are so demanding and bratty.

Well, within two minutes she had everyone eating out of her hand. She was funny, kind, interested in everyone at the table, not the least bit annoyed that this was the one day the kitchen staff chose to be late with everything. I had placed a box of note cards by her place, and she opened it with the same excitement she'd have for a box from Cartier.

I think good girls are sometimes encouraged to overcompensate by being too tough and demanding. Sometimes toughness is the only thing that will work. But most of the time, if the slide carousel is jammed, you'll get the hotel's AV guy to come to the conference room much faster if you graciously ask for help rather than if you throw a hissy fit.

# WHY YOU MUST BE YOUR OWN PR AGENT

Good girls are notorious for hiding their light under a bushel. Every management and communications consultant I've spoken to in recent years has said that the women they work with need to be prodded and pushed into championing their own accomplishments.

Why is it so hard for us to toot our own horns? We've always been told not to hog the limelight and we've been led to believe that if we're good, the right people will eventually notice. Not true. PR whiz Andrea Kaplan says, "You absolutely must promote yourself because if you don't, no one else will."

On the other hand, overselling yourself won't work either. It comes across not only as rude, but even as desperate. You need a more subtle approach.

The trick for any gutsy girl then is to learn to promote herself in a way that gets noticed, but doesn't come across as braggadocio.

- "Write the damn memo": This is an expression used by management and communications consultant Karen Berg. Berg says that no matter how much she encourages women to send memos alerting their boss about their accomplishments, they find excuses for not doing it. Stop hedging or putzing around.
- Be selective. In working with Andrea Kaplan, I discovered that one of her key strategies in promoting stories from the magazine is to be selective. Sure, there may be times when you hope to get something on the AP wire, but there are also nuggets that you offer solely to *Entertainment Tonight*. Giving someone an exclusive not only scores you points, but it can make the item seem juicier.

163

You need to do the same with your own good news. Let your boss know but don't blab it all over, as if you'd just been picked to be on *Jeopardy*. It will not only water down the accomplishment, but it could also provoke lots of envy in your peers.

- Share the glory—but not too much of it. The common wisdom today is that it's vulgar to hog all the glory for yourself. People will be far more supportive of you and happy for your success if you share the glory by using "we." The memo you send starts off with "We did it," rather than "I did it." But, on the other hand, you want to make certain your boss knows the role you played.
- Never say, "I was lucky."

# HOW TO GET YOUR NAME ON THE RIGHT PEOPLE'S LIPS

Personal PR isn't just a matter of trumpeting your accomplishments. You want to pop to mind with the people that matter. In fact, all the strategies I talked about for improving the way you look and sound won't do you any good if you're sitting at your desk. You must be "out there." A few strategies:

- Take advantage of any reason to deal with your boss's boss.
- Work on interdepartmental committees and projects. Jane Hedrick Walter, president of Career Development Consultants in Greensboro, North Carolina, says that it's so important to get visibility outside of your department that if you can't find an interdepartmental task force to take part in, start one yourself.
- Speak to key people in your company at office parties

and conferences. Interestingly, they're often standing alone because employees feel awkward approaching them. Do not, however, put them on the spot by asking about company matters ("Will we really be relocating?"). Instead ask their opinion of industry news and trends that you've been boning up on.

- Get involved in industry organizations, but don't restrict your involvement to mingling and glad-handing at massive cocktail parties. Play a leadership role. Sit on a committee, organize an event, and, best of all, speak on a panel.
- Write a thank-you note to anyone who does you a favor in your business.
- Whenever you get a promotion, send a press release to industry newsletters.
- Write a forward-thinking piece for a company publication.

# MAKE YOURSELF A LEGEND IN YOUR OWN TIME

When I was growing up, there was a memorable and much-parodied commercial on TV for a men's cologne with the tagline, "Give him British Sterling. Make him a legend in his own time."

When I look at so many of the gutsy girls I've known, they've done just that: they've made themselves legends, creating a wonderful mystique about their personalities and their careers. They do this by perpetuating certain "truths" about themselves until an oral history comes into existence and is brought up whenever their names get mentioned.

Sometimes it's all true and sometimes the truth gets distorted—to their advantage. I had a funny lesson in this when I won the *Glamour* magazine contest. The application asked for a list of all the activities I had participated in during college, and wanting to win, I threw in everything I could think of. The last item I put on the list was something called the President's Ad Hoc Narcotics Committee. It was a do-nothing committee, organized by the president of the school, to evaluate how severe the drug problem was on campus. We only met three times, and nothing much was accomplished, but hey, it was something to put on the list.

Three months later I was on the stage at Lincoln Center, hearing myself introduced with the other winners to a throng of *Glamour* advertisers and trade press. And do you know the second thing they said about me? They announced I'd been on the *President's* narcotics committee, as if I'd been tapped by the President of the United States. I wondered if they'd strip me of my title if they found out the truth.

While you don't want to encourage or perpetuate any misconceptions, it doesn't hurt to put your own positive spin on your image. Two little tricks:

# Write a Dazzling Bio of Yourself

There are plenty of times when people require information about you. Perhaps they need an introduction for a speech you're giving or they're doing a profile of you for an industry publication. Over time I've come to see that, if required, they will put that information together themselves, but they are also just as willing to use what you give them—*verbatim*. You should have a bio to send to them. Not a résumé, but a fleshed-out one- or two-page biography that sums up your major accomplishments in crisp, punchy language. Whenever you go to hear a speaker or panel of speakers, you can be pretty sure that the ones who get the best intros are the ones who simply sent over the juiciest bios. And several conference organizers have told me lately that men are far more likely to provide a bio of themselves than women.

## Sum up Your Reputation in a Word and Use It

I heard a speech lately by an editor in my field and she did the most brilliant thing. In discussing why she recently had been hired to overhaul a magazine, she said that she was known as a "rehab specialist." In other words, she went into existing magazines and gave them a new face. I bet everyone in the room remembered that phrase, and you just knew that down the road people would say, "Well she is a rehab specialist." If people come to think of you in a single, powerful word—like rainmaker, budget maestro, idea queen—it will serve you well. It just might be necessary for you to start people along that path.

# CHAPTER EIGHT

# Strategy #6: A Gutsy Girl Asks for What She Wants

I don't think anything has ever been as hard for me as asking for what I want. There were plenty of things early in my career that I yearned for but never had the nerve to request—raises, a better office, a title change—and do you know what helped take the sting out of not getting them? The sheer relief I felt from not having made myself ask.

Asking doesn't come easily to most of us. There's no better evidence of that than Bill Carter's book, *Night Shift: The Battle for Late Night TV*. In it he describes how David Letterman had never asked for a clause in his NBC contract guaranteeing that he'd be given the *Tonight Show* when Johnny Carson retired. There was a clause that guaranteed him $1,000,000 if he *didn't* get it. But he hadn't asked for what really mattered to him. It's shocking to discover this because when you watch David Letterman every night, you assume he's one of the gutsiest guys alive.

Yes, asking for what we want is tough for most of us, including even gutsy girls. But what a gutsy girl accepts that a good girl doesn't is that she must ask anyway. A good girl's first mistake is convincing herself that asking isn't such a smart idea—for two reasons:

1. A good girl feels she shouldn't *have* to ask. She believes that her work stands for itself and she should be rewarded for her efforts without having to draw any extra attention to them.
2. A good girl thinks it looks *greedy* to ask. She believes that those who make demands may get what they want initially, but they are likely to be branded as pushy and perhaps overpriced. A good girl thinks that down the road, such greediness will backfire.

A gutsy girl knows that both points couldn't be more wrong.

# MYTH #1: YOU SHOULDN'T HAVE TO ASK REALITY: THE SQUEAKY WHEEL GETS THE GREASE

One of the most frequent laments I hear from good girls is how disappointed they are over not being fairly rewarded for their accomplishments. A good girl I know was recently passed over for a major promotion, and afterward she told me, "I gave them my *all*, and they ended up handing the job to an outsider."

"Well, what did they say when you asked for it?" I said, trying to get a grasp on the dynamics of her situation.

"I didn't specifically ask for it," she said, surprised by my question. "They know what I can do. They know I wanted it."

This is typical thinking on the part of a good girl. What you've been told over the years is that cream automatically rises to the top. You believe that a boss knows who's doing a great job and who isn't and that when that boss is in a position to do something for the good performer, he won't hesitate. You may even believe that if you *have* to ask for something, you probably don't deserve it.

When you fail to get what you're hoping for, rather than ever consider that it might be because you didn't make your needs known, you start rationalizing. Perhaps, you think, it wasn't within the power of your boss to reward you (budget cuts, top management said to hire an outside person, etc.). Or, you worry, you've overestimated people's respect for your work. Or maybe office politics did you in.

Of course, one of these points *could* be true. But there's every chance none of them are. Your boss may be very pleased with your performance and have the power (and money) to reward you. The only reason he didn't give you what you wanted is that you didn't ask for it.

Now, it's easy to understand why the squeaky wheel gets the grease on a bicycle, but aren't most bosses smarter than that? Isn't it in their best interest to reward the most productive people rather than those with the loudest voices? Of course it's in their interest, but much of the time there are other factors overriding their common sense.

A boss may be stingy. He may be lazy. He may be preoccupied. He may be afraid of upsetting the apple cart of the department by rewarding one person rather than another. He may not realize that you're hungry for a particular reward— or he may have selfishly let events *convince* him you're not, so that he doesn't have to act. Another interesting force that may be at work: He may not like having to worry about your needs. "Sometimes even good bosses don't like being in the role of caretaker, of having to look out for your interests," says psychotherapist Marjorie Lapp. "They're much more comfortable dealing with someone who seems responsible for her own destiny."

Asking is the only sure way to get around any of these problems. If your boss is stingy, lazy, or worried about office dynamics, your asking compels him to consider for the first time that there could be consequences to his passiveness (you could get restless and leave), and he will be forced to take some action. If your boss thinks you aren't hungry for more, you will dazzle him by declaring what you want. If he is preoccupied, this will be his wake-up call.

There is, of course, the chance that your boss really doesn't have it in his power to give or doesn't think you deserve it. But asking can serve you beautifully there as well. If your boss admits that he can't give you money because of budget restrictions, you can negotiate for a better title. If he says you haven't earned a promotion or an assignment, you have the opportunity to explore the perception problems that are hindering your growth.

Now, there will be times in your work life when your boss unexpectedly gives you a bonus, a raise, a promotion, or even a junket to the Maui Sheraton without your ever having had to utter a peep. But consider these fluke occurrences, and do not allow them to lure you into an if-I'm-patient-it-will-come-to-me way of thinking. In fact, when you get handed a surprise perk, consider it a sign that you may not have been asking for *enough* lately and your boss feels guilty. The motto you should live by: *I must ask for everything*.

I got my big lesson in being a squeaky wheel when I was the editor-in-chief of *Working Woman*. I like to call it my $50,000 moment of truth.

One of the reasons I took the job at *Working Woman* was that the owner of the company offered me, in addition to my salary, equity in the operation. At last, I told myself, this is my chance to make some major bucks. I was supposed to receive all the necessary paperwork the week before I started, but despite numerous calls to his office and his lawyer's office, it hadn't arrived by the time I plunked down at my desk on Day One. If I hadn't been such a chump, I wouldn't even have shown up, but my good-girl gland was obviously secreting. Each time I called about the equity papers, I was told that the lawyers were sitting on them. I soon got immersed in the job, and at my six-month anniversary, I realized I still hadn't heard a thing.

This time when I called, I came on stronger, and the papers finally arrived. I sent them for review to my accountant, who happens to be one of the shrewdest guys I know, and within twenty minutes he called to tell me that the deal, as written, would never earn me a dime, and that I'd been crazy not to involve him earlier.

"What am I going to do now?" I wailed. "I promise never to be so stupid again."

"Fine," he said. "I hope you learned from this. Now here's exactly what you have to do. Skip the lawyer. Make an appointment with the owner. Tell him you're extremely disappointed with the vagueness of the equity plan. You need him to get back to you with something far more specific."

"Okay," I said.

"But that's not all. Tell him that because you don't have a clear plan worked out yet, he has to give you something to tide you over. Tell him you want fifty thousand dollars in cash."

"What?" I yelled. "Bob, Bob, Bob, you don't understand. This is publishing. Editors don't do this sort of thing. Besides, the company is cutting back. I'm sure he doesn't even have the money."

"He's got it. Plus, he doesn't want to lose you." He got off the phone telling me that if I didn't do it, I was a wimp.

The whole plan seemed ludicrous to me. Asking for a lump

sum of cash—particularly during a recession—would make me feel like I was living out a scene from *The Godfather*.

But over the next few days, the more I thought about how I'd gotten the short end of the stick, the more I began to lean toward taking action. I didn't think I'd get the money, but asking would make me feel better.

I made the appointment. I wore a great suit. I explained to the owner how concerned I was that I didn't have a viable equity plan. He looked vaguely sympathetic. Then I announced that I would need something to compensate me for not having had a plan during my first year. I looked him right in the eye and said, "What seems fair is fifty thousand dollars."

And you know what? He said okay. He said okay without flinching or squirming or looking irritated. In fact, he looked at me as if I were Barry Diller or Donald Trump.

Which brings me to Myth #2.

# MYTH #2: ASKING CAN MAKE YOU APPEAR GREEDY, OBNOXIOUS, EVEN A LITTLE DESPERATE
# REALITY: BOSSES LIKE IT WHEN YOU ASK

Good girls also have an instinctive fear that asking will reflect badly on them. The message you probably heard again and again when you were growing up was, "Don't speak until you're spoken to." You worry that if you ask your boss for something big, the first question he will ask himself is, "Who the hell does she think she is?" You may even suspect there's a certain pathos connected with asking for what you want. A good girl once told me, "When you have to ask, it's like having to beg."

Forget all of that. Asking not only reflects well on you, it makes your boss look good, too.

If your boss hasn't considered you hungry enough, this alters that perception. But it goes beyond that—you break yourself out of the role of someone who needs to be taken care of. "When you ask for something, you show respect for yourself and that heightens the listener's respect for you," says Lapp.

When you ask, you also reinforce the boss's idea that he's created a vital atmosphere in which to work. I love it when my employees ask to have their roles expanded because it makes me feel that they love their jobs so much that they want *more*.

That said, you *can* seem obnoxious or greedy or pathetic when you ask for something. You have to learn to ask the right way.

## A SMALL WORD OF WARNING BEFORE WE PROCEED: NEVER ASK SOMEONE YOU WORK WITH WHETHER OR NOT YOU SHOULD ASK

Good girls sometimes try to get a handle on whether it's safe to ask for something by sounding out friendly co-workers. This kind of reality check would seem to make sense: Another person can give you an objective appraisal of the situation or even offer information that you may not be privy to. But if you try to test the waters this way, I guarantee that your co-worker will discourage you.

If the person you ask is a good girl, for instance, she'll find a reason even you didn't think of for you to keep your mouth shut. Others may talk you out of an assertive approach because they believe—consciously or unconsciously—that a strong move by you ultimately threatens them. Several years ago, when one of my friends got her first crack at running a magazine, she was upset to discover after she started that her title was editor rather than editor-in-chief. She raised the issue with the editorial director of the company, with whom she'd already established a nice rapport. The woman explained that it had always been standard policy of the company president to start new editors that way. Once the editor had proven herself, earned her stripes, if you will, she'd get the better title. Well, this didn't sit well with my friend, and she said she'd have to talk to the president. Immediately, the editorial director began to dissuade her. "No, no, I wouldn't do that," she said. "It's very important to him to bestow the editor-in-chief title when he feels you're ready. You'll upset him if you ask now."

Not wanting to rock the boat, my friend chose to wait. When the editorial director left the company a year and a half later to start her own business, my friend still hadn't been "bestowed" with the editor-in-chief title, so she worked up her courage to ask the president. He gave her the title immediately, and it was clear from his nonchalance that it had never been an issue with him. She realized that the wait-till-you-earn-it advice had been the editorial director's way of preventing her from advancing too fast.

# THE PERFECT WAY TO ASK

Just about everything I've learned about asking has come from watching some of the dynamic women who sell space in magazines to advertisers. Being by nature a tentative asker myself, I have observed them work their magic—and then I've tried out their strategies in my own life.

According to popular belief, the editorial and sales sides of magazines should never mix. In fact, in the industry they are referred to as "church and state," and it is considered sacrilegious for one side to attempt to influence the other. At the first out-of-town sales conference I attended, as one of three representatives from the editorial side, my boss strongly urged me to steer clear of the sales staff, particularly after dinner. He seemed to be implying that if I wasn't careful, they would get me drunk, take lewd photographs of me, and threaten to pass them around town unless I ran an article stating that cigarette smoking actually healed cancer cells and reversed the signs of aging.

But I found myself drawn to women in sales because of their gumption and joie de vivre, and many of my friends today are saleswomen from various magazines I've worked at.

These are the principles I've learned from them:

# Rule 1: Discover the Other Person's Secret Greed

Before you ask someone for anything, you must figure out exactly what she feels greedy for. Yes, you have your needs, but the way you get a yes is to make the other person feel that it's *her* need you will really be taking care of.

This is often referred to in the world of sales as "finding the hot button," but this tends to sound a little slick. I think it's easier for a good girl to get into the concept if she considers it on more of an emotional plane: discovering what the person wants and providing it. After all, we're trained to please, and we should use that instinct to look for the other person's needs.

A person's secret greed might seem obvious. But you should always do a little detective work to see if there's something operating on another level. Watch, ask questions, snoop around. Once, when I was going through the interview process for a job, I made a few discreet inquiries about the politics of the place and learned that the man I would be reporting to was new, an outsider, and was having trouble with one of the top people on his staff. In my follow-up letter to him I stressed how terrific it would be to be "on his team." I was offered the job, and though I decided not to take it, I later heard through the grapevine that he had lapped up the "team" concept.

My favorite secret greed story involves Caroline Kennedy. Soon after I got to *McCall's*, we put together a special section on women who were making big strides in the nineties. On a long shot we called Caroline Kennedy, who had just coauthored a book on the Bill of Rights, and much to our surprise she agreed to a short interview on the subject. As the editor was leaving my office, I yelled out, "Would she be on the cover?" That, I knew, would be a major, major coup. Caroline Kennedy practically never gave interviews and she had *never* posed for the cover of a major women's magazine.

"No way," she said.

"How do you know?" I asked.

"I just know," she said. "It's clear from talking to her that she wants to keep a low profile."

"So then why did she agree to the interview?"

"She wants to publicize her book."

Ahhhhhh, there was the hot button. I told the editor to tell Kennedy that we would put the name of her book on the cover if she would pose for it. Two days later she agreed. We were the first woman's magazine ever to have an authorized picture of her on the cover (and it jumped off the newsstand).

Want to hear something amazing? The good girls who work for me usually do a lousy job of finding my secret greed. When they do ask for something, they often talk only in terms of their *own* needs. "I think I deserve this." "I want this." "I need this."

This isn't just my observation. Nancy Hamlin, president of Hamlin Associates, which helps organizations deal with gender issues, says that over the years she's frequently seen women fail to put themselves in their boss's position when they're making a request. "They focus on *their* needs but not the needs of the other person," she says. "Before you ask for something, you have to create a blackboard in your mind with your needs on one side and your boss's on the other. You must address each side—so both of you will feel satisfied."

Why, if a good girl feels a compulsion to please, does she take a self-absorbed approach when asking? This used to baffle me, but I think I've finally come to understand the reason. Good girls feel uncomfortable acting as if the other person's needs are more important than their own when that really isn't the case. And they believe it's basically . . . well, *evil* to flatter, fawn, or tell a guy that it would be terrific to be on his team when he's really about as exciting as a Pendaflex folder.

If your conscience is preventing you from pushing someone's hot button, keep this in mind: people generally find it delicious to be flattered and schmoozed, and they rarely hold it against you. Besides, if you end up meeting their needs or relieving their headaches, they will be very, very grateful.

## Rule 2: Ask Fast

When you go in to make your request, quickly and clearly spell out what you want. In the height of my good-girl days I always felt a need to do a warm-up, to "prep" the listener with lots of background and explanation, as if doing so would protect me from a hasty no. But I've come to see that this kind of hemming and hawing only bores, irritates, or confuses the listener.

Before you go in to ask, crystallize everything you want into one clear statement of purpose. Then rehearse it. Start with a hit to the secret greed and then make your point. ("Sandy, I know how disappointed you must be about Tom leaving. He did such a terrific job for you on the budget. I'd like you to consider me for the role of budget director because I believe I can be the kind of watchdog you need and also offer some innovative programs that would help you save even *more* money.")

# Rule 3: Sell Yourself Hard

This can be tough, even for gutsy girls. Adele Scheele says that over the years she's counseled people about their careers, she's seen that across the board women have a harder time than men selling themselves and talking up what they do. "Men talk about their jobs as if they own the company," she says. "Women, on the other hand, will talk about their jobs as if they are several notches *below* where they actually are on the corporate ladder. It's almost a taboo for women to brag about their work."

And yet that's what you're going to have to do. You're going to have to give the reason or reasons you deserve what you're asking for.

Because talking about your accomplishments is awkward for you, you may end up sounding vague or unconvinced of your own worth. (I-think-I'm-really-good-at-what-I-do kind of statements.) A good strategy is to pick three or four succinct points about yourself and relate each directly to a criterion for the job or promotion.

## Rule 4: Ask for the Business

This is an expression I'd always heard salespeople use. It sounds straightforward enough, but there's a little twist to it that I didn't get until I applied for the job of editor-in-chief of *Child*. The final in a series of interviews was with the two top people on the business side of the magazine, including the publisher. After I'd talked to them for about forty-five minutes, the conversation began winding down and I was afraid it would end with a fizzle. The moment called for something creative and bold. As they shifted a little in their seats, I leaned forward and said that I wanted to add just a few words in closing. I told them that I'd enjoyed the whole interview process, that I thought I would make a terrific editor based on A and B, and that I wanted the job very much. The publisher announced, somewhat briskly, "We hear you," and that was it.

As I left the office, I was worried. Perhaps I'd come across as too slick at the end, too much like an infomercial pitch for a $198 skin-care regimen. Was the "We hear you" remark a sign of annoyance, I wondered, or just the publisher's no-nonsense way of talking? A few weeks after I got the job, the publisher and I had lunch and we ended up chatting about the hiring process. "You know what sealed the deal for you?" she said. "You asked for the business."

Asking for the business really means being absolutely sure you've asked. Too often salespeople do a lot of schmoozing and present a lot of facts, but never come right out and pop the question. So just to be safe, ask one final time—and do it with gusto.

And I mean gusto. A friend of mine called me recently to say that she was one of two finalists for a major editor-in-chief job. She should have been happy, but she had a bad, nagging feeling. Because she was already the editor-in-chief of another magazine, she hadn't thought it behooved someone in her position to act like an eager beaver, so she'd played things cool. Now she was worried she'd been *too* cool. The next week the job went to the other candidate, who my friend later heard had pitched herself as if the fate of Western civilization depended on it. People want you to seem passionate about what they are passionate about.

# NOW THAT YOU'VE ASKED, DON'T SAY ANOTHER WORD

This is a trick I learned from Cheryl Brown, a friend of mine who is associate vice president for university development at the State University of New York at Buffalo. Brown has spent twenty years at schools like UCLA asking people to donate major philanthropic gifts, and she taught me that as hard as it is, you have to ask and then "let them say the next thing." Too often, she points out, we ask and then immediately feel the need to apologize for asking or to modify our request.

I think good girls, in particular, feel the urge to jump in and save the person from what they're asking for. You say you want an assistant of your own, but before your boss can answer, you announce that you would settle for a college intern twice a week. Though it may seem like a millennium, let the silence work for you.

Of course, if you pause and the other person begins squirming as if you've backed him into a corner, switch gears and give the experience some closure. You can say, "I know you'll probably need some time to think about this," and depart gracefully.

# THE SINGLE BEST THING TO ASK YOUR BOSS FOR: MORE RESPONSIBILITY

Yes, you want more money and yes, you want certain perks. But one of the most important things you should be asking for on a regular basis is more responsibility.

In Chapter 3, I mentioned that one of the most effective rule-breaking strategies is to expand the parameters of your job description/title. There are bosses who will notice your talent and reward you with job-expanding opportunities, but much of the time you have to come right out and ask for them.

Please notice that I've been using the word *responsibility* rather than *work*. That's because it's easy for good girls to fall into the trap of simply taking on lots of extra maintenance work, not unlike cleaning the backboards. What you want are projects that provide you with more experience, more knowledge, more skill, more clout, more exposure to key executives. These will dramatically bolster your value.

In a recent study, top executives were asked, "What do you feel is the single best way for employees to earn a promotion and/or raise?" Eighty-two percent said asking for more work and responsibility, compared to 11 percent for publicizing achievements and 2 percent for working longer hours. (Good girls, please take note of the very last part!)

What you really want is enough additional responsibility to provide you with a whole new specialty or area of expertise that you can leverage. It's far easier to go from VP of nuts to VP of nuts and bolts if you've already taken over the bolts. In the Korn Ferry study of executive women, over half of the respondents said that taking on "different functional responsibility" was one of the factors in a particular breakthrough or turning point that put them on the path to success. Consider this story that happened to an acquaintance of mine:

She was the articles editor of a women's magazine. Her job entailed overseeing every article that ran in the magazine, with the exception of short lifestyle articles on fashion, food, and beauty. These were the province of her counterpart, the lifestyle editor, a shrewd, ambitious woman. Each month the lifestyle editor would send my friend, as a courtesy, an updated list of features she'd assigned, things like "How to Get Rid of Stubborn Stains" and "Sponge Painting for Beginners." My friend would give it a cursory glance, sometimes letting out a hoot as she saw the topics. Over time, however, she began to notice that the list was not only growing in length, but the subject matter was also expanding. There were now pieces on investing and budgeting, as well as self-help articles on building self-esteem. This was a clear invasion of turf.

"I suddenly could see that she was like an amoeba," says my friend. "She was swallowing more and more of my responsibility."

By the time my friend went to the editor-in-chief to complain, it was too late. The editor-in-chief wasn't going to curb the lifestyle editor's new specialty because she was happy with the results. Shortly thereafter the lifestyle editor got a bigger job, leveraging her new area of expertise.

I tried to sympathize with my friend. But the truth is that I couldn't help but secretly admire the Amoeba Woman's style.

One nice little bonus about asking for more responsibility: it's one thing bosses *really like* giving because it doesn't make them feel they've been depleted in any way.

# THE SECOND-BEST THING TO ASK YOUR BOSS FOR: AN UNPLEASANT TASK YOUR BOSS IS STUCK WITH

Though you don't want a diet of go-nowhere projects, you should occasionally volunteer to take a crummy job from your boss. Like the slide show he must put together on trends in refrigeration. This will score big points for you.

# THE IMPORTANCE OF ASKING FOR WHAT ISN'T AVAILABLE

One of the most fascinating things I've noticed about gutsy girls is that they're good at not only asking for the obvious, but also at going after what others might assume isn't up for grabs. They ask for a company car even though no one else has gotten one. They ask to create an interdepartmental task force even though there's never been one before. And lo and behold, they get what they ask for.

Whereas good girls are programmed to think, Oh, they'd never do *that*, a gutsy girl knows that it never hurts to ask.

# THE YUCKY PROBLEM OF ASKING FOR MONEY

There's asking for what you want, and then there's asking for money. To a good girl, the first seems tough but the second is positively excruciating. As a good girl, what you may do to avoid having to talk raw numbers is to convince yourself that good bosses pay you what you deserve. Wrong. They pay you what they can get away with. As a friend of mine in human resources says, "When we get someone cheap, we think how *lucky* we are."

A gutsy girl knows that the only way to guarantee that she'll earn the money she wants and deserves is to go after it aggressively. When she starts a new job or gets a promotion, she negotiates for as much as she possibly can. *But that's not all.* She also realizes that getting the money she wants isn't a once-a-year experience at salary review time. A gusty girl thinks of her salary as a living, breathing thing that she must constantly manage—almost as if it were a stock portfolio. She must, for instance, keep her eye on the market (if she's been at a company for a while, she may not be keeping pace with the industry—even though she's getting decent raises). And she must find innovative ways to grow it (by asking for bonuses, perks, etc.).

Any discomfort we experience when it comes to asking for money may reflect messages we got from our parents. A 1993 study of 600 college students by Jerome Rabow and Michael Newcomb of the sociology department of the University of California, Los Angeles, found that parents' expectations for their male and female children about money differ dramatically. Sons, more than daughters, perceive and evaluate their parents as expecting them to know how to work and to save. Males are introduced to discussions of family finances at an earlier age than females, are more likely than women to work in college, and receive less financial support from their families than females do. Such differences, in expectations and behavior, help establish what the researchers call different money "tracks" for males and females.

As a long-term result, say the researchers, men and women have sharply different evaluations of money in relation to themselves and others. Men, more than women, feel positive about money and others who make money. Men feel that those who earn money are rational, responsible, and attractive. Money makes men feel lovable, happy, in control. Women, on the other hand, are repelled and intimidated by money and consider those who earn good incomes immoral.

*Repelled* and *intimidated* are pretty strong words. They make it sound as if our attitude toward money is pretty ingrained. Now, I hate to quibble with the people from UCLA, but I have my own theory on this subject. I think that, yes, some women *are* uncomfortable about money matters, and maybe they even start out thinking money isn't so nice. But I also believe that the first time you can afford to buy a pair of Calvin Klein gabardine trousers with your income and compare the beautiful, silky feel of them against your thighs to that of the partially polyester ones you purchased from T. J. Maxx, you cease being repelled by the concept of money. In fact, you find it quite a lovely thing. From there, all it takes is a little behavioral modification to learn how to ask for more of it.

# First, Determine What You're Worth

One of the mistakes good girls make when they discuss salary with a boss or potential boss is not having any sense of their actual value in dollars. Therefore, they end up accepting a salary or raise based not on their worth but on guidelines from Human Resources or on somebody's budget or simply on what they *were* making ("I'm making X now so I should ask for Y.") If you follow any of these approaches, you are likely to end up with far less than you deserve and even far less than what they might be willing to give.

To determine your worth, you must consider both the market rate for your position in the industry and your performance in your current job.

For market value, you have to keep your ear close to the

ground and listen for tidbits about what people in your field and in your company are making. Over time, I've found that office and industry rumors about salaries are like *National Enquirer* stores about JFK Jr.'s love life: They may be somewhat inflated but they're based on a nugget of truth. In other words, don't dismiss them.

I've also been bold enough to quiz people. I would never ask anyone's actual salary (though I would if I thought they'd tell me), but I've asked peers whom I know in the industry what they feel is the going rate for the position that we're in. They won't give an exact amount, but they'll offer a range, which can be very revealing. How do I know they're not lying? Well, here's my theory: I don't think they lowball the number because they don't want you to think they're making a skimpy salary. And they don't highball it because they wouldn't want you to go out and ask for more than they're making.

Next you need to figure your value to the company. In some areas, like sales, it's easy, but in others it's tougher to quantify. Do your best to calculate your value based on the business you've brought in, the projects you've created or executed, the money you've saved the company.

## Now Increase That Number by 20 Percent

Good girls are notorious for deflating their value, so this offers you the necessary padding.

## Let Them Name the First Number

Even though you've got a number in your head, generally it's best to let them go first. That's to protect yourself from coming in lower than even what they had in mind.

# Always Ask for More—Even if They Say Your Number

That's really an unpleasant proposition, isn't it? Good girls worry that if they ask for more, they'll damage the rapport and trust that's been established. As a friend of mine says, "You're afraid they're going to yank the offer right out from under you for being such a brat to want more."

And yet, as my guru in human resources reveals, "they" always have more than the number they give. And they go in expecting that you might ask for it. A study we mentioned in *Working Woman* found that 80 percent of the time those who asked for a bigger raise got it.

# Use the Phrase "I'm Looking For . . ."

When you *do* ask for more, avoid pleading phrases like "I really need . . ." or demanding ones like "You have to give me . . ." "I'm looking for" is a nice neutral statement.

# THE GUTSY WAY TO TAKE A NO

Sometimes, no matter how beautifully you've asked—whether it's for money, or more staff, or more responsibility—you will be told no. Never simply accept a no and proceed to the door with your tail between your legs.

# Scenario One: They Claim You Haven't Earned It

If the no appears to be based on a problem with your performance ("I don't think you're ready for that kind of project," or "We feel someone from the outside could bring the kind of fresh thinking we need," etc.), you should use this as an opportunity to ask questions and explore exactly how your boss views you and your work.

To a good girl this is about as appealing as renting a house alone in the woods, leaving the back door open, and watching *Night of the Living Dead*. Why terrify yourself? A gutsy girl knows, however, that in the long run, whatever discomfort she feels will end up paying off for her—it's her chance to improve her performance or change a misperception. Ellen Abramowitz, who was the ad director at *Working Woman* and is now the advertising director of *Seventeen*, always used to tell me, "You can't be afraid of the bad stuff. When you listen to the negative things they're saying, you translate it into something you can accomplish."

Though you need to know the bad stuff, you don't want a bloodbath. That's not only unpleasant for you at the moment, but it can also cast a pall over your relationship with your boss. The key is to hear the negative in a positive way. You can do that by using a strategy I learned from one of the best publishers I ever worked with. Whenever the magazine didn't win a piece of business from an advertiser, rather than ask, "Why don't you want to advertise with us?" she'd say, "What do we have to do to get the business next time?" The focus, then, became "What can we do right?" rather than "What did we do wrong?" Use that same approach. Instead of saying, "How come?" or "Why not?" ask, "What do I have to do to make it happen?"

Be careful not to sound antagonistic or defensive. The more information you elicit, the better. You should follow up with a memo explaining how you will accomplish all that's been discussed.

## Scenario Two: They Want to But They Can't

In many instances you will be told no not because you don't deserve it, but because outside forces are tying your boss's hands. He may say something like, "You definitely deserve more money but I just don't have it in the budget right now," or "I'd love to let you go to the conference this year, but it wouldn't be fair to Joe or Stacey." Some bosses will masterfully try to play on your good-girl sympathy or guilt, taking you into their confidence about all the problems they're facing. When I was at *Working Woman* the owner told me he couldn't let me have a car service because we were in the middle of a recession and it would upset the four people in the accounting department to see that I was getting that kind of perk.

There's a chance that your boss is being truthful, but it could also be total BS. Look sympathetic but *do not give up*. And I don't mean to start bargaining for some kind of compromise situation. You still have a chance to get what you want. Your boss may simply be seeing if he can take the wind out of your sails, knowing from experience how easily people capitulate.

Before you give up hope, try this: *the broken record technique*. When I was writing consumer rights articles for *Glamour*, this is a strategy that a consumer advocate taught me for dealing with difficult store clerks, airline agents, etc.—and I have used it religiously ever since.

The basic idea is to repeat your request like a broken record, without ever changing your tone so that your emotions don't appear to be escalating. For instance, when an airline agent insists that he has no record of your reservation, rather than throw a tantrum, you repeat over and over, "I know I made the reservation and I must be on that flight." It really works.

Try the same approach with your boss: "I understand that there are budget restraints and I know how much pressure we're all under, but I hope my efforts can be rewarded."

# HOW TO WALK AWAY WITH SOMETHING

If the broken record doesn't get you what you want, you don't have to go away empty handed. Now you're ready to negotiate. You want to walk out with something, even though it's not what you first had in mind. Bosses actually like it when you try to bargain because they feel less guilty. For instance:

- If you're told you're too junior to receive a new responsibility, ask for a trial assignment.
- If department guidelines won't allow for more than a 4 percent raise, ask for a spot bonus.
- If they swear the budget absolutely won't allow for a promotion, ask for a title change, with a raise to come when the freeze is over.

# TRY, TRY AGAIN

As I've talked to gutsy girls, one theme emerges over and over again. They never give up after hearing no.

It may seem like you're a nag, but people are flattered by your desire to connect with them or impressed with your hunger and passion.

# TWO THINGS A GUTSY GIRL NEVER ASKS FOR

I've been talking about all the things you must demand, but there are two things you should never go in search of: (1) praise; and (2) unnecessary advice.

When you go fishing for compliments you seem needy. When you ask for unnecessary advice, you can open a can of worms, forcing your boss to give you criticism or duties you don't really want.

# WHY TAKING IS ANOTHER FORM OF ASKING

A variation on asking for what you want is simply taking what you want. Now, there are plenty of things that aren't appropriate for you to take because they are someone else's to give. But there's a gray area of projects and perks that don't belong to anyone in particular. Asking would be awkward or draw undue attention, so you must simply assume ownership. If you don't, someone else will.

Good girls are terrible at taking because they believe that anything highly desirable must actually belong to someone else or they assume there is some reason why they aren't supposed to have it—and they will get their wrist slapped if they make a raid on it.

The first great lesson I learned in taking was when I won the *Glamour* contest. Part of the prize was having our photographs taken for the August issue of the magazine. All the winners would appear in fashion spreads and one lucky girl would be chosen for the cover.

Now, I wanted to be on the cover in the worst possible way.

As a gawky, dateless teenager I'd read Jean Shrimpton's book *The Truth About Modeling*, and fantasized about being a cover girl one day. This was my one shot at fulfilling my old fantasy.

So when it came time for us to select the clothes we would wear from a giant rack of fall fashions, I did something that seemed to me perfectly malevolent. As all the other girls chose shirts and sweaters in the muted earth tones that were popular that year, I made a beeline for the bright yellow sweater that had "cover look" stamped all over it (even though I never wore yellow myself). As I saw one girl after another pick a dull-as-dishwater sage cardigan or burnt sienna pullover, I wondered guiltily if I should point out to them that magazine covers were traditionally bold and colorful—but I kept my lips zipped. Even now when I come across that old cover and see my face smiling up at me in the yellow turtleneck, all I can think is, You little conniver.

No guy would think that way. Men are the masters of taking what's there for the taking—and they never, ever feel apologetic about it. When I was at *Working Woman* I hired this fabulous male senior editor, the only male editor on the staff, who was brilliant at taking. About five months after he joined the staff, our company hit some tough financial times and we were forced to leave our halfway decent office space and move to recently vacated space in another building. It was the pits. The walls were filthy, the carpet looked as if it hadn't been cleaned since 1957, and the space was so tight that four senior editors, including Mr. X, were going to have to share a large rectangular room that was once the library—and oh, their assistants were going to have to sit in there, too. These, by the way, were all editors who had had their own offices at our previous address.

The day of the move was chaotic, with workmen not only moving in our stuff but removing lots of old furniture that had been abandoned by the previous tenants. The managing editor stopped by my office periodically to fill me in on all the moaning and groaning the editors were doing about their fate. Around midday she raced in and announced that I had to come down and see what Mr. X had pulled off.

As his female colleagues had unhappily unpacked their boxes, he had been busy getting the lay of the land and greasing the palms of workmen. He had managed to secure a freestanding bookcase that he used to wall in his end of the room, as well as a clubby little couch. By the end of the day he had created a comfy office all to himself. It almost appeared as if he were the boss and the female editors were the typing pool.

Never assume that just because no one has grabbed something that it's not yours for the taking. If there's an empty seat next to the big cheese at a meeting and no one is sitting there, go ahead, help yourself.

# NINE ....................................

# Strategy #7: A Gutsy Girl Faces Trouble Head-On

The first time anyone tried to sabotage me at work was a chilling experience, in part because it seemed to come out of nowhere—and from a person I liked.

I had hired this woman myself, for a special project, and because I was overloaded with work, I gave her plenty of autonomy. I did, however, pop into her office periodically to see how things were progressing. She was pleasant and smart and we got along well. Eventually the project came to an end and my boss and I decided that we would absorb her into the main operation, where she would be reporting directly to me.

That's when the trouble started. She didn't like having to answer to me, perhaps because we were the same age, perhaps because she thought she was more capable than I was. Whatever the reason, she bristled when I top-edited her work and she was snippy to me at staff meetings. I decided not to say anything to her, convincing myself that her discontent would burn off in a few weeks as she got used to the change in procedure. But things only got worse. I heard through the grapevine that she was complaining about me to the younger people on the staff, some of whom suddenly developed a weird coolness toward me. A little voice inside told me that I had to take the bull by the horns, and yet I was afraid if I confronted her she would simply accuse me of being paranoid.

One day, two people on the sales staff asked me out to lunch and said that they had a serious situation they had to speak to me about. They explained that this woman had now taken her complaints about me outside of the editorial department. "She's trashing you to anyone who will listen," one of them said. "And because she seems so sweet, people assume she must have a case."

Needless to say, I didn't feel much enthusiasm for my chicken paillard after their revelation. In fact, I lost my appetite for the rest of the day. The problem was not only bigger than I had imagined, it seemed bigger than I could contain. Obviously, it had flared up when I began putting "controls" on her, but it was surely more complicated than that—or else she would have simply come to me or my boss and complained. Bad-mouthing me to everyone indicated that there were other issues. Was she jealous of me, angry that I had the bigger job and she didn't? And even if I could now find a way to deal with her rage effectively, she had already done some serious damage to my reputation. As they say, when someone throws mud, a little of that mud always sticks to you, even if you didn't deserve to get hit.

That night, as I lay in bed unable to sleep, I did allow myself one moment of consolation. I told myself that at least I would never be so naive again. At least I was now armed with the fact that as you go through your career, you are bound to work occasionally with someone who will try to get you.

Unfortunately I couldn't have been more wrong.

You see, what I have learned in subsequent years is that my 2:00 A.M. revelation was a good-girl way of seeing the world. What a gutsy girl realizes is that there are not simply a few bad people out there who will try to derail you. Every single person who crosses your path is a potential saboteur. You must be ever vigilant—and when you spot trouble, you must confront it.

# WHY EVEN NICE CO-WORKERS BECOME BARRACUDAS

With so much emphasis on teamwork these days, you may wonder how I could have such a negative attitude. Aren't we all working together now, cheering each other on, taking pride in each other's accomplishments? That does happen, of course, but let's not let all the happy talk mislead us. In addition to the fact that there are more than a few real nasty types out there disguised as team members, some of the nicest, well-meaning people will undermine you if the right conditions are created in the work ecosystem. And they may not even be aware on a conscious level of what they're doing.

There are two conditions under which people are most likely to become your saboteurs: (1) they're incompetent at the job they're currently doing; or (2) they feel threatened by you.

## The Boss Saboteur

During my twenties, whenever a friend of mine complained about her boss and used the sentence "I think she's threatened by me," I always reacted as if she had told me that a UFO had landed in her yard. I'd try, as a good friend, to sound concerned and supportive, but part of me was always highly skeptical. How could an experienced, accomplished boss feel endangered by a twenty-five-year-old, even if she *was* a go-getter? Then one day I experienced the same sentiment about a boss of mine—and I silently asked forgiveness of those friends I'd classified as delusional.

If higher-ups are going to you directly or responding more enthusiastically to your ideas than your boss's, he can indeed feel threatened by you, but it's not always as straightforward as him sitting up nights in his BarcaLounger downing gin and wondering when management is going to kick him out of his nice big office and award it to you. What he may experience instead is a seeping discomfort or irritation. Even if he feels totally secure in his position, your talent and energy can make him question his own, making him feel like an imposter who may one day be exposed.

How does his fear manifest itself? He may keep you out of meetings you should be part of, co-opt your ideas, cut you down to size in front of your peers, and limit your access to those higher up. A thirty-four-year-old friend of mine has recently had this problem with her fifty-four-year-old boss. She took over an area in the company that he only loosely supervised and as soon as she started to shine, he began to reduce her power and steal her thunder. She was due to make a presentation of her department's accomplishments to top management and her boss suddenly announced that he would give the first half of the presentation. My friend had no choice but to go along, and they rehearsed together over the next week. The day arrived and the boss delivered his half of the presentation. My friend started to rise for her portion, and then watched, with jaw dropped, as her boss simply barreled along, giving her part of the presentation as well. Later, when she asked for an explanation, he told her he wanted to spare her the stress.

A boss can also sabotage you with his incompetence. A bozo boss casts a halo that can make you appear incapable, too. A boss who is talented in his field but lousy at delegating will threaten your chances of developing expertise you critically need.

## The Subordinate Saboteur

In many respects subordinates can be the most dangerous saboteurs because we are less likely to suspect them or worry that they endanger us. After all, we have "authority" over them, and thus we shouldn't have to be concerned.

The most obvious danger is from incompetent players on your staff. They, of course, not only jeopardize matters by making mistakes and mishandling critical situations, they also suck the energy out of you and force *you* to pick up the slack they create. Good girls seem to have a special blindspot for incompetent employees because they hope for the best with people and then don't want to do anything "mean." I once had a good girl on my staff who hired a person under her who turned out to be a disaster, and in the end I lost as much faith in the good girl as I did in her hire. First there were the months of denial, in which the good girl kept saying that she knew her staff member would blossom as she became more familiar with the process. Then, once the problem had been acknowledged, there was the procrastination, I think because the good girl didn't really want to do the dirty work. By the time the incompetent member had been transferred to another area, the good girl had sustained almost as much damage in my eyes.

Your subordinates can also feel threatened by you, though that's something we rarely think of. There are a few obvious situations. You take over a department and everyone there seems to hate you for what you might do to the status quo. But your employees will also feel anxious and threatened if you fail to give them adequate responsibility and autonomy or you offer no sense of direction. They will then sabotage you by performing poorly, complaining about you to one another as well as other people in the company—or resigning in the middle of your biggest crunch.

# The Peer Saboteur

Peers, to me, are the trickiest saboteurs because our relationships with them are less formalized and we don't have any real control over what they do. Unlike with subordinates, you lack the right to challenge their behavior, and unlike with bosses, it's not expected that they might tell you what's on their minds.

In some cases peers will be threatened by your very existence, by the simple fact that you're smart, energetic, and could end up getting the promotion they want. After I began writing major features at *Glamour*, one of the hot writers in the department, who was just a few years older than I, took me aside and said she had something important to tell me. She said she'd been thinking about my future and knew exactly what I should do. I sat there with a little grin on my face, knowing that she was about to say something sweet to me, perhaps that I was destined to be an important magazine feature writer. But to my astonishment she announced, "I think you should consider running for Congress."

Later, I realized I should have been flattered. She didn't just want me out of the magazine, she wanted me out of the *industry*.

Sometimes a peer feels threatened by a specific move you make that bugs the hell out of them. I once had a terrific relationship with a peer, until, that is, I was awarded a special project by our boss. From that moment on she seemed supremely irritated by everything I did and actually presented two ideas I had shared privately with her at a meeting—as her own.

Threatened peers may respond by turning cool on you, stealing your ideas, belittling you in front of people, boxing you out of activities, or launching a back-stabbing campaign like the one that happened to me.

With more and more companies setting up team projects and team decision-making, an incompetent peer can also pose a danger to you. She may fail to perform a function effectively that has a direct bearing on what you do.

# THE #1 RULE OF OFFICE POLITICS

Everything there is to say about dealing with office saboteurs can be boiled down to one simple principle: You must do *something*. I say simple, and, yet, that's exactly what a good girl doesn't want to hear. As a good girl, you most likely hate confrontation. It's awkward, it's embarrassing, it's terrifying. In some cases you may end up in a state of denial, convincing yourself that a situation isn't all that bad. Or you may recognize that you're under attack, but simply choose not to take action. New York City management consultant Karen Berg says that she often consults with women on how to confront a co-worker over a sticky situation. They'll work out a strategy, agree on a plan, but when she asks two weeks later if the woman followed through, the answer, she says, is often, "Well uhhhh . . ."

Once a good girl makes a decision that she's not going to take action, an interesting dynamic begins to take place: She convinces herself that not acting actually was the best strategy. Sometimes, she tells herself, it's best to allow things to sort themselves out.

She may go so far as to talk the situation over with a friend, which, unfortunately, creates the false sense that she's done something about it. One recent study on women and anger showed that, despite myths to the contrary, women don't suppress their anger about situations with spouses and co-workers. They do, however, fail to express it *directly*. Only 9.6 percent of the women in the study said they expressed it directly to the person who caused it. About 81 percent expressed it to a third person.

As a former good girl, I know how easy it is to convince yourself that a bad situation will go away on its own if you just let it. The truth is that unconfronted issues fester, intensify, and sometimes even explode. Also, when you allow someone to get away with bad behavior, you give them permission to do it again. Poachers will poach again, back-stabbers will stab again, and the person who stole one little idea will begin to plot a million-dollar heist.

I had a funny little lesson once in how things only get worse if you try to ignore them. The editor-in-chief I was working for at the time invited me to join a monthly planning meeting that she and two other editors participated in. It was clear right away that each player had her own "seat" at these meetings. The editor-in-chief occupied a chair, the executive editor sat on the short end of an L-shaped couch and the third person, who was on my level at the magazine, sat on the long end of the L. The obvious place for me was on the other half of the long end of the couch. But my peer had positioned herself more than midway down the couch, with all her papers between her and the other editor, so there was only a small space for me at the end. I took the seat anyway, since there was nowhere else, and I figured that once the meeting got going she'd scoot down. But she didn't. I rationalized that she hadn't known I was coming and that at least at the next meeting she'd leave me more room, but no, it didn't happen. In fact, as the months went by, she seemed to take up even *more* room. By the fourth meeting she was saving me space the width of a lasagna noodle. I had everything I could do to keep from falling off the couch.

You're probably wondering why I didn't do anything about this ludicrous situation. Well, I eventually I did, but not for six months, and that's because I kept telling myself it would "work itself out." It wasn't until I sat there one day with one cheek on the couch and one in midair that I realized that it was not only unlikely to get better, but there was every chance it would continue until the day I found myself sprawled on the floor.

What did I finally do? I stopped being a total wimp, got to the next meeting early, and plopped myself down in the middle of the couch. I can't tell you how shocked this woman looked when she saw me there, but after that there weren't any more "squeeze plays." Looking back, it's a pretty silly episode overall, but it drove home the message for me that things, unfortunately, just don't go away. You've got to take action, no matter how distasteful it may seem.

## PRACTICE PREVENTION POLITICS

Now at this point you may be starting to squirm. The idea of constantly having to confront and handle lots of sticky situations doesn't sound very appealing. But before you get into confrontational mode, I have some good news. There are several steps you can take to minimize the number of these situations you have to face. A gutsy girl knows that it's always best to curtail any sabotage before it occurs.

# Take the Temperature

Because so many problems fester, the best strategy is to catch them at the very early stages—or, even better, before there's enough going on to create a flare-up.

A gutsy girl knows she routinely has to take the pulse of her department, even when everything looks perfectly normal. The gutsy girls I've talked to find excuses to pop into people's offices, chat with them, pick up subtle clues about what's going on.

Pepper Schwartz, who is professor of sociology at the University of Washington, says that she finds it helpful to develop a "theory" about each person she works with. "I know what makes them tick, what their needs are, what their weak points are. That makes it easier to pick up on nuances and spot when things aren't operating correctly."

You've got to do this even with your boss. Good girls feel reluctant to "manage" their boss because they don't think that's their job. But so many bosses are bad people-managers that you have to take over the responsibility. You should be asking for input, setting up regular meetings. If you have one of those bosses who really does want to give people a long rein and hates seeing your face constantly at his door, you must still set up a way to get regular feedback and exchange information—a bimonthly meeting, for instance.

If you do sense there's an itty-bitty problem brewing, don't follow the good-girl "wait and see" tack. I know it may seem foolish to draw too much attention to an issue when there's a chance it will blow over on its own, but over time I've learned that it's always best to act early. Say, "Something seems to be on your mind. Do you want to talk about it?"

# Tell Them What They Want to Hear— Even the Bad Stuff

One almost sure way to cause co-workers to misbehave or turn on you is to deny them information they want and are entitled to. People experience a compelling urge to know anything that affects their fate, including the negative. When I was first working as an articles editor, one of the good-girl mistakes I made was holding back bad news from those who worked for me—for instance, that their idea had been turned down—because I felt uncomfortable telling them and I convinced myself that a few more days of ignorance was bliss for them. But I eventually learned that being in the dark made them cranky, irritable, sometimes borderline murderous.

My friend Stephanie Cook, senior VP, Bloom FCA, a New York ad agency, says that she lives by the principle that "people want to know what side of the boat to row on."

Be straight with them and don't make them wait endlessly for the facts. If you do, they may find ways to go around you.

# Consider the Old "Two to Tango" Principle

Sometimes when people feel threatened by you, it is not simply because of your brilliance and energy. Rather, it's because you are doing something to scare the bejesus out of them.

Take for example the boss who seems bothered by your successes. He sends a curt note reminding you to get all your memos approved by him before sending them out. Or he sees you lunching with his counterpart in another department and gives you the icy treatment for the next two days. You need to ask yourself, Can I blame him? Why, for instance, would you not have bothered to get his okay on memos? Why would you have lunch with a possible rival of his without telling him? It's time to start acting as if you're part of his team.

# Reshape the Situation to Your Advantage

Sometimes—not always, but sometimes—you can recast a relationship with someone so that it doesn't become adversarial. It takes a fair amount of guts to do this. That's because you must always take the initiative—it won't happen on its own and the other person isn't likely to do it. And you must practice a little humility. It's amazing who you can turn a potential adversary into: a confidante, an adviser, a team member.

Consider the silly sofa shenanigans in my own past. What I should have done was to imagine what the dynamics might be at the first meeting I attended. Because I knew that my peer had a tendency to be overly sensitive to anyone on her turf, I would have realized that she might react in a defensive, threatened way. What I could have done is drop by her office several days before the meeting and attempt to *shape* the situation differently. She was a very nurturing person, so I might have said something like, "As you know, I'm going to be attending the planning meetings, and I'd really appreciate your help. Can you tell me a little bit about how they work?" She would have been flattered to have been asked and I would have thanked her generously for filling me in. Then, at the meeting, there's every chance she would have gone out of her way to make me feel included—and she would have certainly given me more than two inches of fanny space.

Someone once said to me that even the most Machiavellian people have fears, and if you can get to that fear first and allay it, you may short-circuit bad behavior.

If there's any time when you must attempt to shape a relationship, it's when you get handed a new boss. A new boss is almost always going to approach you with caution, even skepticism. Because of her mind-set, she may even misinterpret innocent behavior on your part. There may, for instance, be certain tasks your old boss allowed you to handle autonomously but when you continue following that procedure, the new boss assumes you're going behind her back. That's why you must set the tone of the relationship as much as possible as soon as possible. Offer to help and to share information so she sees you as her ally rather than an enemy.

## WHEN IT'S TIME TO TUSSLE

Of course, all the preventative work in the world doesn't guarantee that you'll be able to avoid having someone try to sabotage you at some point. If that's clearly happening, it's time to take action.

Yes, I know the idea of confronting another person at the office is a dreadful proposition, and yet if you approach it in the right way, it may not have to be so ugly. The best way to start, actually, is to get the word *confrontation* out of your brain. Yes, you want to confront the situation, but with the individual involved you ideally want to have not a confrontation, but a *conversation*. You want to discuss the problem in a reasonable way and find a resolution.

Interestingly, that's not something women have been encouraged to do in recent years. In order to get out of the rut of being too nice, we've been told to assert ourselves, play hardball just like guys do. And yet what I've discovered over the years is that the most effective men in business play a form of Nerf ball instead of hardball. They take aim, they get their point across, and yet no one suffers a concussion.

"One of the observations I've made about many of the career women I counsel," says psychotherapist Marjorie Lapp, "is that they often take a very forceful or shrill approach to expressing their anger or discontent because they've been told they ought to be more assertive. I call it the Attila the Hun syndrome. Yet in many situations, a diplomatic approach works much better. That's something many men seemed to have learned."

Though it may run against the get-tough messages you've been told in recent years, it's always best to win without bloodshed. In *The Art of War*, written two and a half thousand years ago, Sun Tzu advised, "To fight and conquer in all your battles is not supreme excellence; supreme excellence consists in breaking the enemy's resistance without fighting."

If the problem is with a subordinate, you should call him into your office, close the door, and present the situation in a firm, direct way. If the infraction is grievous, you may be tempted to yell or even berate, but that won't get you what you want. It won't make an ignorant employee smarter and it certainly won't motivate anyone capable of doing better. A far more effective approach is to express your disappointment and let it hang in the air.

At this time your subordinate is likely to offer an explanation and you should listen carefully. Even the lamest excuses sometimes contain a nugget of information that points to action on your part that may be facilitating the problem. Insubordination, for instance, sometimes results from a lack of direction and feedback.

How you wrap up the conversation depends on how complex the problem is. If your assistant has been coming in late each day because of boyfriend problems, you simply remind her that the day starts at 9:00 and she must adhere to that schedule. In more complicated situations, you can get terrific results by challenging your employee to help you work out the solution himself. ("How do you think we should handle this situation?")

With your boss, you must be much more delicate. Management consultant Kathy Strickland says that she finds that an excellent technique when confronting a boss is to express confusion. ("For the past month, I've noticed you've asked Sandra to sit in on the marketing meetings, but not me. Since that's my area of expertise, I'm a little confused. Can you clear this up for me?") Confusion shows concern, and puts your boss on notice if he's trying to pull a fast one, but it doesn't sound accusatory.

With peers it can be dicier. If the situation is black and white, it's easy to call a spade a spade. When someone once stole an idea of mine, I walked into his office and told him not to do it again. And he didn't. But you're often dealing with fuzzier stuff—perhaps you've heard that a co-worker has been complaining about your research, and yet there's no proof. Unlike a boss or a subordinate, a peer is under no obligation to play fair with you. If you bring up your grievance, there's every chance he will look at you incredulously, as if you've just accused him of being behind the JFK assassination.

A little confusion can work here, too. You can tell your peer what you've heard, indicate that such behavior isn't acceptable but give him the benefit of the doubt. ("Someone took me aside today and said you'd been complaining about me. That doesn't sound like you. I hope that if you have any sort of grievance you would come directly to me.") That not only opens the opportunity for discussion, but serves as a warning.

Career strategist Adele Scheele once gave me a wonderful tip about handling a peer who has been poaching or backstabbing. Take notes during your "discussion" with him. It's amazing how that prevents future problems.

# AND ALWAYS GO ONE-ON-ONE

Always try to solve the situation directly with the person, rather than involving your boss, human resources, or six people you're friends with along the corridor. It's not simply that the person will respond better if you don't appear to be a tattletale. When you complain about someone, the person you're complaining to will always assume that you are partially responsible for the problem, and may even consider you a troublemaker. Years ago I had a problem handling a young woman who worked for me. I should have spoken to her directly, but we were the same age, and I felt awkward, so I went to my boss and complained about her. He waved his hand dismissively and announced, "I'm not going to get in the middle of the battle of the blondes." At that moment in his eyes I was on about the same level as a female Jell-O wrestler.

# SHOULD YOU EVER BLOW A GASKET?

The idea of being diplomatic doesn't offer much relief if someone has tried to take advantage of you or has damaged you because of their ineptness. What you really want to do at a time like that is let them have it. A ballistic approach certainly can be satisfying—at least during the moment and for the first five minutes afterwards. But then you're left to pick up the pieces.

What you have to decide ultimately is whether blowing a gasket will get you anywhere. Dr. Peggy Saylor, who helped conduct one of the largest studies of women and anger, says that she always advises women to ask themselves, Is it in my best interest? "It might make you feel good momentarily to call him an SOB," she says. "But in the long run, going over-board with your anger may not serve you well."

## THE HIDDEN SABOTEUR

It's not just people who can sabotage you. There are also cer-tain *things* that can act like land mines to your getting your job done—a confusing hierarchy, poor interdepartmental communications, a lack of back-up help, inadequate technol-ogy.

Good girls often are befuddled and immobilized by such things, even more so than by human saboteurs. But you must confront this kind of trouble as well. Assess the problem, con-sider the possible solutions and then ask for what you need.

## MEN AT WORK

Just after my boss at *Family Weekly* left to become editor-in-chief of *GQ*, one of the top guys in the sales department sat down with me and another woman on the staff and discussed some fun things we might do for the going-away party. "Oh, I gotta great idea," he suddenly announced. "You know how much he liked you two. You could both put on falsies and pa-rade up and down in front of him."

Rather than feel offended, I left the room laughing to my-self. The times they were a-changing, and I knew that a guy like that was a dinosaur, on the road to extinction.

Every successful woman I've talked to admits how much more comfortable life is with men in the workplace compared to what it was like when they first started their careers.

And yet that doesn't mean there aren't still problems. Dis-crimination exists, hostility exists, harassment exists. According to a 1992 Korn Ferry study of executive women, 59 percent have experienced what they consider to be sexual harassment.

The most common situation I see these days isn't out-and-out hostility or harassment, but rather something I call guerrilla chauvinism, or what Mary Rowe, a labor economist at MIT, describes as "microinequities" and "microaggressions." It's a very subtle form of discrimination, sometimes intentional, sometimes not, that's very tough to deal with because it's so subtle and slippery.

"Microinequities are woven into all the threads of our work life," reports Rowe. "They are micro not at all in the sense of trivial, but in the sense of miniature."

They can take many forms, from a male co-worker making a disparaging remark about you to your boss excluding you from the golf outing to management arranging for belly dancers to perform at the sales convention. In some offices women get labeled in demeaning ways. Management consultant Nancy Hamlin says she was called in to consult with a company in which the three top women were referred to as "the good girl, the bad girl, and the bulldog."

With some forms of guerrilla chauvinism, you may not even be sure you have a justifiable gripe. One minute you're convinced you were purposely left out of a meeting, the next you're wondering if you're overreacting. You're like the heroine in a movie in which your husband is trying to make people believe you're losing your mind so he can collect your fortune.

Even when you're certain there's been a slight, intentional or unintentional, you may feel silly raising the issue. I had a male boss who was absolutely terrific but wouldn't make eye contact with me when he was in a meeting with me and another man. In these situations the third party would invariably pick up on the exclusion and before long, he would ignore me, too. I worried that if I ever said anything to my boss, he'd look at me as if I'd announced that Elvis was hiding in my office.

And that's the kind of thing that *does* happen when you raise the issue. They act as if you're paranoid, lacking in humor, or overly sensitive. A friend of mine once had a horrible male boss who loved to take little digs at her. She was having lunch with him and a client one day and the topic turned to diets because the client had ordered her salad without dressing. My friend, who looked terrific, had lost thirty pounds over the course of the previous year, but she chose not to say anything about her own weight loss because she didn't consider it appropriate. Her boss, however, announced, "You should have seen Patricia last year. She was a three-hundred-pound porker." When my friend confronted him about it later, he said, "Can't you take a joke?"

This guy was the devil in disguise, but I believe many men simply are ignorant. They want to do the right thing but they've never learned how. I'm not an expert in this area—what woman is? But here are a few things I've found that work for me.

## Say Something

Trust me, it won't go away if you ignore it. Now you may expect that I will suggest a verbal lashing for the perpetrator, but that won't get you what you want. Recently I saw some sample dialogue in a magazine about how to handle a male harasser, and it was pretty tough stuff: you were supposed to admonish the guy and threaten to take it to the top. Though you may be totally justified to fight fire with fire this way, and it will make you feel good too, you could easily burn yourself in the process. Jane Hedrick Walter, president of Career Development Consultants in Greensboro, North Carolina, says,

"You have to avoid being offensive. You may be within your rights, but I feel a woman has to remind herself, 'If I offend, I'm dead.'"

## Where Possible, First Try a Little Humor

Not everyone feels comfortable with this approach, but it's a natural response for me, having grown up with five brothers, and it often gets the job done. You put the guy on notice that he's stepped over the line, but you have also let him see that you will not exact a penalty—not now, at least. There's that great moment in *In the Line of Fire* in which Clint Eastwood, a fifty-plus Secret Service agent, says to Renee Russo, "The secretaries get prettier and prettier around here," even though he knows she's an agent. Rather than bristle, she lobs one back: "And the field agents get older and older."

The trick is to be funny in a way that doesn't encourage his behavior. My strategy is to make my remark humorous but leave off the smile. A man in my former company ran into me having breakfast in the lobby of a hotel he'd been staying in, though we weren't in town for the same business. Across the room he yelled, "You kept me up all night banging on my door trying to get in." With a glint in my eye I said, "I hope you're not interested in being on the Supreme Court some day."

## Try Firm, Not Feisty

If you feel uncomfortable with humor or feel the situation doesn't call for it, put the guy on notice with a firm, totally neutral comment. ("We have a good professional relationship and I want to keep it that way.") Don't make any threats. As an old friend of mine in human resources says, "We are *all* defensive, and if you come on too strong, you're going to make him feel backed into a corner. The goal is to stop the behavior, not put up a barrier."

You should avoid labeling the behavior and cast your statement primarily in terms of how you feel rather than what they did. Instead of "You made me feel like a fool when you brought out the belly dancers," go for, "I felt uncomfortable when the belly dancers came out." Or instead of "You always exclude me," "I'd love to be part of the golf outing." Not only does that sound less antagonistic, but you give them less room to declare your perceptions to be invalid or worthless. You may not know what's in their mind but you know what's in yours.

At this point, you may feel you want to take your case to your boss (assuming he isn't the harasser) or the human resources department, but for the time being use them only in an advisory role, to help you with strategy and dialogue. If you tell the problem person that the situation is already in the hands of human resources, you'll only antagonize him. If you fail to make progress with him, that's when you need to take the matter officially "upstairs."

## Include Them

Jane Walter says that women have "exclusive patterns" too. The more you invite men into your activities and share ideas with them, the more likely they are to reciprocate. And the better the chances that they'll see you as a human being, not as a bulldog.

# WHAT TO DO WHEN A GUY TRIES TO BOX YOU OUT

Guys, even nice guys, are notorious for running over female co-workers in meetings. You try to make a comment and your male colleague repeatedly interrupts you. Or worse, you present an idea, no one seems to hear it, and then your male colleague presents it ten minutes later to the raves of your boss.

You need to take a gutsy stand when this happens. But you also should realize that the guy may not be totally to blame. Good girls often sit in meetings as if wearing a sign that says, "Go ahead, walk all over me."

## First and Foremost, Never Present Your Million-Dollar Ideas at Group Brainstorming Meetings

It's too easy for people to forget where they came from. You should present them in writing to your boss or in person with written back-up, so there's always a paper trail. If your boss prefers that big ideas are presented in meetings, always introduce yours with fanfare. ("Bob, I'd like to present an idea that will allow us to cut our research costs in half.")

## Don't Whisper

In certain instances, people act as if they didn't hear your idea because they *didn't*. One woman executive told me that when she saw a videotape of herself at a meeting, she realized she brought up ideas in a tiny voice—and suddenly it was no surprise to her why she hadn't been heard.

# Lean In

There's some fascinating research that shows that men tend to lean toward the center of a group's communication process far more than women do. In addition, women tend to lean *away from* the center. The study also revealed that the more involved an individual is in terms of body lean, the less likely he or she is to lose their speaking turn due to interruption. Because women are less likely to be involved, they're more likely to be interrupted.

# If You Do Get Boxed Out, Don't Make the Problem Worse by Beating a Retreat

Often, when men try to exclude us from events or interrupt or dismiss our remarks, we respond by pulling back, sinking into our seat, or withdrawing into the woodwork. Or we go the other way, acting shrill, desperate to get a word in.

Instead, get calmly back into control. One trick I've found helpful for meetings in which a guy is trying to run over your comments or hog the limelight is to ask a question of the key person and create an exchange between just the two of you. That gets the ball in your court without making you look desperate. Management consultant Karen Berg says she saw a woman reclaim her power in a meeting by standing up and walking around the table as she made her comments. All eyes were totally focused on her. Another technique Berg recommends for letting your presence be felt: Be the one who sums up what's been said and where everyone should go from there ("It seems, then, that we should . . .").

# SEX AND THE WORKING GIRL

Up until this point, it seems that all I've talked about are the not-so-pleasant things that can happen when you're working with men. But as we know, lots of nice things happen as well. Male co-workers can be fabulous teammates, supporters, advisors, mentors, and champions. They can also be flirters, lovers.

I once had a loud verbal disagreement with a well-known career expert who'd written a piece for me saying that you should never ever get romantically involved with someone you work with. To me it was like saying you should never ever eat butter. Unrealistic advice—and extremely *boring*.

According to a recent study there's a 60 percent chance that you will go out with someone you work with. At the very least you may flirt with a co-worker or experience some sexual tension that goes nowhere but creates an exciting work environment.

A gutsy girl is realistic enough to know that hormones can work overtime at the office but she proceeds cautiously in these matters. Even an "innocent" flirtation or relationship can end up sabotaging her.

Here are some statistics of my own.

1. Even if you're only engaging in harmless office flirting, there's a 40 percent chance people will start spreading the fact that you're "involved." I once interviewed someone who was doing his dissertation on rumors. His theory was that rumors are simultaneously sloppy and precise. They may not be true but they're based on a factual nugget: This is how a flirt can turn to dirt.

2. No matter what you do to conceal a romantic relation-

ship with a co-worker, there's a 95 percent chance that your other co-workers will find out.

3. If he's married or you're married or he's your boss or you're his, know that there's a 75 percent chance that a relationship could turn into a big ugly mess. And a woman, no matter what her rank, still ends up with the worst part of such a mess.

4. Even "innocuous" relationships—he's in a totally different department and is on your level—there's a 25 percent chance it will somehow be used against you.

## THE MOMMY ISSUE

It probably won't surprise you to learn that as a mother of two young kids, I have some pretty strong views about being a working mother. Though combining kids and career isn't for everyone—and I very much respect my friends who've bowed out of the race for a few years—I also believe you can pull it off under the right set of circumstances.

That said, there are also lots of chances to get sabotaged. You may have absolutely no interest in being on a mommy track and yet you find you've been put on one anyway— you're given wimpy assignments or excluded from A-team meetings. It's even possible to sabotage yourself, without even realizing it.

But I do think I can offer a few pearls of wisdom about handling matters at the office. It's the result not only of learning from my own mistakes, but also of listening to one of my oldest friends, Judsen Culbreth, who has been the editor-in-chief of *Working Mother* for seven years.

First, I think you have to take a really gutsy approach to being a working mother, which means plotting, planning, and sometimes grabbing the bull by the horns. Because working moms don't like to draw undue attention to their situation, they sometimes operate in a reactive rather than proactive mode and let their fate unfold.

The most proactive thing you can do, Culbreth has taught me, is have a job that you love—and from there, things are much more likely to go in your favor. "Study after study we've done shows that the women who manage to make it all work are those who have the least ambivalence about their jobs," says Culbreth. "It's as if a domino effect takes place. If you love your job, for instance, you're more likely to stay in touch when you're on maternity leave, and that not only keeps you in control, but it signals to your boss that you're truly committed."

The boss you have also makes a critical difference. "The best boss for a working mother, our studies show, is a working mother," says Culbreth. "The next best is a man whose wife is a working mother. After that, it goes downhill. These are only generalizations, but it's helpful to be aware of them."

What about everyday issues that working mothers face? Should you keep your kids' pictures on your desk? Should you admit that you're tired because your four-year-old had the croup and you spent almost the entire night monitoring the humidifier and trying to help her stop barking like a seal? A lot of that depends on your own workplace, and you're going to have to learn to be your own gauge. Culbreth says that in many workplaces today being a parent is no longer viewed as a negative, but as a sign that you're a well-rounded person— and that means parents are able to be more candid. But proceed cautiously. It never hurts to err on the side of maximum discretion.

In some respects, I feel that worrying about how many pictures of your kids you should keep on your desk doesn't get to the heart of the matter. All your boss is really concerned about is how committed you are to your job, and you must aggressively let her see that you are and reassure her if she's in doubt. If, for instance, you leave at 5:00, as I do, let your boss know that you put in another hour or more after your kids go to bed.

## RUMORS, GOSSIP, AND LIES, OH MY!

There is one other big way you can get sabotaged at work and it's getting worse these days. People will break your confidence or they will spread rumors about you, both true and untrue.

Everything about the state of discretion in the workplace can be summed up in this remark an acquaintance made to me. She had just had an interview with a woman recently named editor of a magazine. My acquaintance mentioned that the new editor planned to fire many of the employees at the magazine.

"I'm surprised she would confide that to you," I remarked. "Isn't she worried that you would tell people?"

"Well, she asked me to keep it confidential," she said. "And other than you, my two roommates, and my boyfriend, I haven't told a soul."

That is exactly how you can expect people to respond if you ask them to keep a secret.

A good girl trusts people. A gutsy girl knows that you can never, ever completely trust anyone. Never tell a secret to anyone without knowing that there is every chance it will be betrayed.

And what if people simply choose to start a rumor about you?

Frankie Sue del Pappa, the attorney general of Nevada, who is known as one of the gutsiest women in politics, says that you must shut a rumor down. "There was a time when it might have been best to leave it alone. If you drew too much attention to it, you might make it worse. But those days are over. It will snowball until you address it and say that it's wrong."

# CHAPTER
# TEN ......................................

# Strategy #8: A Gutsy Girl Trusts Her Instincts

Though I had been the editor-in-chief of two magazines before I went to *McCall's*, in many respects I'd been playing in the minor leagues and was now moving up to the majors. *Child* and *Working Woman* had 250,000 and 900,000 readers respectively; *McCall's* had 5 million. On the newsstand *Child* and *Working Woman* each sold considerably under 100,000 each month, whereas *McCall's'* average sale was about 400,000.

One of the scariest pieces of information thrown my way the first week on the job at *McCall's* was that the newsstand sales could fluctuate by several hundred thousand copies each month, depending on who and what was on the cover. The wrong instinct about a celebrity could cost thousands of dollars. It seemed hard to believe, but women like Dolly Parton and Princess Di were now in a position to make or break my career.

My job started in March and commitments had already been made about the July and August covers (Sally Field and Andie MacDowell, respectively). For September I was on my own. I stared at a long list of women provided by the enter-tainment editor. There were the usual suspects: women of substance, women of substance abuse, those whose hearts had just been broken, and those who were triumphantly on the mend. Absolutely no one excited me.

Sometime over the next day or two, I had a brainstorm: what about Demi Moore? She was absolutely gorgeous, a mother-to-be, and she had just starred in the runaway hit *Ghost*. In fact, I was surprised to discover that none of the major women's magazines had yet featured her on the cover.

Well, I soon found out why. Demi Moore didn't pose for magazines like *McCall's*, thank you very much. I'd had my heart set on her, however, and I didn't want to give up the idea. I suggested to the photo editor that we call in as many recent paparazzi shots as possible because we didn't need the star's permission to use one of those. Though there were often slim pickings among these kinds of photos, occasionally you'd stumble upon a shot good enough for a cover. Two days later the photo editor called me down to look at a selection on the light box, and there, among the various shots of Demi as a brat-packer and Demi as a sexpot, was a drop-dead picture of her in a low-cut black evening dress with husband Bruce Willis, partially in the picture, whispering in her ear. Her eyes were moist, her skin dewy, and she had the slightest of smiles, almost like the Mona Lisa. It practically took my breath away and I decided in that instant, "This is the cover."

Over the next few days, we retouched the photo slightly, evening out the skin tone, removing both Bruce's three-day beard and a clunky necklace on Demi. As I showed the blown-up photo around the office to staff members, people began to raise concerns. Demi didn't have the typical big, "buy-me" smile our cover subjects usually wore—was that a turn-off? Besides, the background of the photo was black, more like an old *Modern Screen* cover than one for *McCall's*.

Then a wrench got thrown into the works. A gossip columnist announced that a pregnant Demi would appear nearly naked on the cover of *Vanity Fair* in August, just one month ahead of our issue. I began to wonder if Demi might be too controversial and the picture too "different." I took the photo into my office, closed the door, and just stared at it. All I could remember was the "oooooh" reaction I'd felt the first moment I'd set eyes on it. I decided to go ahead.

Well, the issue sold 300,000 more copies on the newsstand than the September issue had sold the year before. I think it was in large part due to the pure beauty and appeal of Demi, but we probably also rode the tailwind of curiosity and desire created by *Vanity Fair*'s now-legendary shot of the pregnant star. There were probably people who mistakenly bought *McCall's* thinking they would find nude photos of Moore inside.

The Demi cover experience was a great lesson for me. Though I'd certainly relied on my gut in making creative decisions before, this was the first time it had such a quantifiable impact. But I learned something else as well: how easy it is to get talked out of going with your gut when the pressure is on—and that's especially true if you're a good girl.

## WHY GOOD GIRLS ARE SCARED TO TRUST THEIR INSTINCTS

Good girls feel uncomfortable going with their gut or trusting their instincts because often it means going against what other people think. What a good girl wants is consensus. When she gets consensus, it not only means that she's managed to please everybody—a high priority—but that she's guaranteed herself safety in numbers. That's exactly what I was hoping for with the Demi Moore cover, and I felt disconcerted when I didn't get it.

Also, a gut reaction by its very definition is something that comes from someplace other than your brain, involving intuition rather than lots of analyzing. Good girls have been trained to believe that they must always do their homework. They may have a hard time trusting a reaction that isn't obviously based on lots of facts and figures—or, even worse, is *counter* to the facts and figures.

"As females grow up, they're not encouraged to believe in their perceptions or observations," says social psychologist Allana Elovson. "People talk about women's intuition, but we're often ridiculed for it. When we do use our intuition and we're right, it's attributed to luck or hard work instead."

And yet learning to trust your gut is essential for anyone in business. The gutsy women I know all say they rely on their gut to guide them. A New Jersey Institute of Technology survey found that 80 percent of those company leaders who had doubled their company profits in a five-year period had above-average powers of intuition.

Why is it so important? Because if you allow yourself to be overwhelmed by constant analysis, lots and lots of rules, and the negative vibes of people who react to a great idea as if it's a bad smell, you may never pursue the boldest, most creative, rule-bending way of doing something.

More and more research shows that women may actually be capable of greater accuracy in their gut reactions than men. Anne Moir, Ph.D., and David Jessel, authors of *Brain Sex, The Real Difference Between Men & Women*, point out that women have superiority in many of the senses, which makes them better equipped at picking up social cues, such as important nuances of meaning from a person's tone of voice or intensity of expression. According to the authors, women also can store, for short periods at least, more irrelevant and random information than men. And that's not all. In one study it was discovered that the two sides of the brain, connected by the corpus callosum, have a larger number of connections in women. This means that more information is being exchanged between the left and right sides of the female brain. The *Brain Sex* authors conclude that since women are in general better at recognizing the emotional nuances in voice, gestures, and facial expressions, they can deduce more from such information than men because they have a greater capacity to integrate and cross-relate it.

This may be how the notion of women's intuition developed, although, as psychologist Dr. Allana Elovson says, that "asset" is often ridiculed or considered operative only in silly matters, such as knowing that your long lost cousin is about to call from Phoenix.

A gutsy girl recognizes, however, that her gut is a powerful tool and she learns to listen to it. How does she know when it's talking to her? She may feel a rumble or knot in her stomach if something isn't "quite right." When she's got a winning idea, there's a rush of adrenaline or a buzzing in the brain, or perhaps even a weird "sixth sense." In an article about Tina Brown, *Vanity Fair* contributing editor Kevin Sessums says that Brown knows that an article is right if her nipples get hard when she reads it.

# HOW TO DEVELOP A GOLDEN GUT

You probably feel nervous about letting go of your data sheets and operating on gut instinct. Here, then, is a beginner's approach. It will allow you to learn gradually to develop your gut—with a safety net in place.

# Go Ahead, Do Your Homework

As a good girl, one of the reasons you probably feel anxious about relying on instinct is that for years you've been told to do the opposite. You've always been instructed to study hard, get all the facts, and be prepared. Using your gut seems like winging it—or even cheating.

Well, the truth is that a good gut reaction often comes from having done your homework, from having enough information at hand that an idea feels right for a reason.

"A lot of the time, intuition is actually a groundswell of the experience you've had and the information you've learned over the years," says Mother's Work president Rebecca Matthias.

Take the Demi cover. My initial reaction to that photograph was influenced by information I'd already learned. I had recently read several articles about what was happening to *Ghost* at the box office. It was an unexpected megahit, one that was attracting almost double the number of women than men— and many of them were seeing it more than once. Several "experts" had hypothesized that its success reflected a desire for romance in films as well as a need on the part of many people to be reassured that there might be some form of immortality. Based on the success and the theme of the movie, it would make sense that a tender, almost mysterious shot of Demi could work—perhaps even better than one with a glamorous, megawatt smile.

When Claire Brinker first suggested to management at Red Cross Shoes that they ought to create and market a walking shoe, her gut feeling about it was backed up with plenty of research from places like the U.S. Park Service showing that walking was booming as an activity. And unlike many leisure activities, it appeared to have staying power. "I had demographics on my side," says Brinker. "As women aged, they would be even more likely to want to walk because it's kinder to an older body. Plus, research showed that people like to walk not only because it's good for their hearts and their cholesterol levels, but it's mentally relaxing." That fact seemed to promise that many women would be walking long after they had sold off their Thighmasters and Abdomonizers at tag sales.

The best gut instinct is always an educated one. When I first got to McCall's, I thought I could use my gut instinct "as a woman" to judge every idea, but I soon realized that in some ways I was different from the McCall's reader and a pure gut reaction didn't work. I have a real irreverent streak and an appreciation for saucy women—if it were up to me, Sharon Stone would be on the cover at least once a year. But it soon became clear that McCall's readers didn't have much appetite for sauciness. They liked a straightforward approach and women who were loaded with integrity. When I put Priscilla Presley on the cover with lots of exquisite cleavage, several readers complained, including one who said she was horrified that her mailman now assumed she was the kind of risqué person who subscribed to dirty magazines. I had to educate myself about the reader.

So go ahead, bone up, get the numbers, make the analysis. The trouble good girls have with homework is that they can do too much and end up in a *paralysis of analysis*. Or the homework offers contradictory information and they're not sure which road to head down. It's at this point that you have to go into your office, close the door, and listen to your instincts.

"You can't overanalyze," says Matthias. "At some point you have to step back and ask, 'Would I and my friends, as consumers, want to buy this?'"

After launching and running a highly successful chain of maternity clothing stores, Matthias wanted to open another chain that also sold maternity clothes, but more upscale outfits. Not everybody thought it was a good idea. And Matthias knew there were plenty of case studies around demonstrating how a second business can cannibalize the main one. "But I always felt that there were two kinds of shoppers for maternity clothes," says Matthias. "There was the Talbot's shopper, whom we were attracting with Mother's Work. But there was also the upscale Barney's shopper, whom we *weren't* yet marketing to."

Matthias went with her instincts and Mimi's was born, geared to upscale mothers-to-be. Matthias says it has been a ringing success and has not hurt the original chain.

Note, by the way, the use of the word *felt* on Matthias's part. For me, this has always been a way to sort out what my gut is really telling me. If I'm considering a step that sounds good "on paper," I ask myself how I *feel* about it rather than what I think of it. In other words, if it makes me feel energized and excited, that's a much better sign than merely thinking it would be "important" to do. If I'm still in doubt, I ask myself, How will I feel if I *don't* do it?

I've always wished I'd done this with my Warren Beatty cover. After I'd been at *McCall's* for a few months, someone on my staff suggested him for a cover and I said yes because I thought it would make us look sophisticated and trendy. But if I'd asked myself how I *felt* about Beatty I probably would have answered, "The guy's a dirty old man." That cover was my all-time biggest dog as far as sales.

# Beware the Good Girl's Favorite Circuit Jammer

There are plenty of impediments to intuition, but a good girl often gets sidetracked by one in particular: *what everybody else thinks*.

Because a good girl likes pleasing people and not causing any controversy, she may allow herself to be talked out of a good idea just to create consensus (or talked into a bad idea for the same reason). She may even talk herself out of a good idea because she doesn't want to fight the tide.

At this point you have to use what I call the Body Heat test. When I was working at *Family Weekly*, a major part of my job was to recommend the celebrities for the cover, so I went regularly to screenings of upcoming films. One night I found myself sitting alone in a dark room watching a new film called *Body Heat*. It wasn't a perfect movie. The music was overblown, the plot was somewhat convoluted, and everyone seemed to sweat more than they should have, considering that air conditioning had already been invented. But I was mesmerized. There was heart-thumping suspense, very sexy sex, and Kathleen Turner saying things like, "You're not too smart. I like that in a man." Did I suggest that we immediately do an article on William Hurt or Kathleen Turner? No. Because two people from work who had sat in front of me snickered about the movie as they left the theater, making me question my original impression. The film was a huge hit and turned both actors into major stars.

Today, when I have to make a judgment and lots of people have thrown in their two cents, I always give myself the Body Heat test—I try to get back to my very first feeling about the idea before anyone else said a word.

Claire Brinker says that when she thinks about some of the

projects she's worked on that haven't been a success, they're generally those that she let other people talk her into, even though she had bad vibes initially.

The other trick, of course, is simply not to ask people. Certainly it can pay off to ask the people who have insight and brilliant judgment, but get over the good-girl tendency to include others just to be polite.

# Strip Off All Your Clothes and Run Naked Down the Street

I don't mean that literally. What I'm talking about is getting yourself in a certain state of mind—a creative state of mind. You see, a golden gut isn't only one that tells you that A is a better approach than B. It's also one that's capable of coming up with C, a bold, new approach that no one has considered before. And in order to produce C ideas, you must loosen up, strip away your inhibitions, and let yourself have some fun.

There are lots of wonderful techniques for unleashing your creative instincts, but there are two that are especially helpful to good girls.

First, you have to give yourself time off to relax. You take enormous pride in how hard and how long you work. In fact, it may be well over a year since you've even had a vacation. Maybe they really can't live without you, but never giving your brain a rest provides no time for great ideas and revelations to germinate, percolate, or do whatever they do so well at a subconscious level.

Rebecca Matthias makes sure she gets a twenty-minute bath every night and forty-five-minutes of reverie outdoors on a bench every Saturday, just for relaxing and reflecting.

Some of the very best ideas occur when you're in a dreamy

state, when you've pushed budget restrictions, cost analysis, R&D reports, sales projections, and organizational tables out of your mind.

Interior designer and author Alexandra Stoddard told me a story once of how she and a team of people from her book publisher had tried fruitlessly for days to come up with a cover concept for her newest book. Finally, she put the project out of her mind. She and her husband were traveling a day or two later, and while she sat in the airport, she daydreamed about her home in Connecticut, which she and her husband had just lovingly restored and which she now longed to return to. Suddenly, the idea for the cover came to her. "As I sat there daydreaming I could see the front of the house with its two pillars on either side of the door," she says. "And I thought how charming it would be to have the book cover look like that, with two pillars on either side."

There's another kind of loosening-up good girls need to do in order to be more creative, and that's daring to think about the situation in a different way or from a totally different angle. In Chapter 3, I talked about how a gutsy girl makes her mark by breaking the rules, by taking a step that's outside the parameters of her job or the outlines she's been given for a specific project. You also have to break the rules in the way you think. Roger von Oech, who is president of Creative Think, a California-based consulting firm, and the author of *A Whack on the Side of the Head*, says that creative thinking requires an attitude that allows you to manipulate your knowledge and experience. Sometimes, he told me, it helps to "use crazy, foolish and impractical ideas as stepping-stones to practical new ideas."

Be playful, silly, outrageous. At *Working Woman*, we once interviewed a team of people who had created a successful new shampoo by asking themselves, If we were a hair shaft, what would we want? Jonas Salk is said to have used a similar approach when he was frustrated in his quest for a polio vaccine. He asked himself, If I were an immune system, what would I do to fight a virus or cancer cell?

Over time, I've come to see that some of my best ideas are generated when I do what I call "reading upside down." By that I mean that I look at a piece of information from a different angle or focus on a teeny-weeny aspect of it. For instance, when I was at *Working Woman*, editors were always suggesting that we do cover stories on Christie Hefner, president of *Playboy*. She was young, beautiful, and was one of the most powerful businesswomen in the country. I felt, however, that there'd been an overabundance of coverage on her. One day an editor made another stab at it, sending me a proposal for a profile, with a few clips attached. As I took a cursory glance at the clips, my eye fell on this little nugget buried in the middle of the story: 47 percent of the people in management at *Playboy* at that time were women. How could they feel comfortable there? I wondered. And that was the birth of one of my favorite articles, "Why Would a Smart Woman Work at *Playboy*?" It was a provocative piece that looked at how women rationalized working for a magazine that ran nude pictorials of their "sisters" with titles like "Animal Attraction" and "Leggy, Bosomy and Hot Blooded: The Birds of Great Britain." We even ran the story on a centerfold in the magazine.

# FIVE WAYS TO KNOW WHAT PEOPLE WISH YOU DIDN'T

Working in a creative field, it's probably been easier for me to learn to trust my gut with ideas than if I'd worked in, let's say, the insurance industry. In the magazine industry, you're constantly encouraged to go with your instincts, and anyone with a golden gut is revered. I've had a much harder time trusting my gut with people.

For years my good-girl tendency was to believe that there was basically something good about everyone. When a co-worker pulled a stunt that seemed mean, malicious, or under-handed, my initial instinct was to give that person the benefit of the doubt. I'd think, *She's just preoccupied*, or, *He's having a bad day*. There were sparks that turned into brush fires because I didn't acknowledge to myself that the situation was combustible.

I once took over a job in which one of my new subordi-nates began giving me a hard time almost from the start. I told myself she was just getting used to the change. Plus she had had bronchitis for several weeks after I started and I figured that she felt out of the loop. Even when I developed bronchi-tis several weeks later and she announced in what seemed like a high state of glee, "I hope you didn't get it from *me*," I told myself that maybe I'd misinterpreted her tone. Months later I learned that she had wanted my job and was immensely an-noyed by my appointment. I finally woke up to the fact that the woman couldn't stand my guts. (At that point I even had to wonder if she'd sneaked into my office one night and pur-posely sneezed all over my desk.)

Why does a good girl think this way? Psychotherapist Mar-jorie Lapp says that a good girl tends to believe that the same principles that apply in a friendship apply at work. When someone's behavior appears malicious or incongruous, she gives that person the benefit of the doubt because she doesn't expect unfairness, mean-spiritedness, or betrayal.

Or, Lapp says, the good girl wonders if *she* has done some-thing wrong, which only serves to distract her from noticing what's really essential. A good-girl friend of mine told me, "I once came across two people whispering in a stairwell and au-tomatically assumed they were whispering something negative about me. A month later the company was sold—that's what all the whispering was about. While some people were getting their résumés together because they'd picked up on the clues, I'd been wondering, Why don't they like me?

Of course, some things *are* meaningless or coincidental, so you don't want to overreact. I went to work once for a very mercurial woman who had previously employed a friend of mine. My friend's advice: "Sometimes she's going to seem really cool to you, and you're going to panic. But give it twenty-four hours. She might just have had a bad haircut."

Because I tend to err on the side of seeing the rosy view, I've adopted these tactics:

# 1. Look a Second Time at Anything You Just Dismissed

The moment you hear yourself pooh-pooh anything ("Oh, he's probably just in a grouchy mood," or "I'm sure that will never happen"), immediately backtrack and review the event or remark. What *could* it mean? What are some of the implications? What's the worst possibility? I know that sounds paranoid, but because your good-girl tendency may be to rationalize when an event makes the hairs on the back of your neck go up, it's smart to revisit it and get your fears "on the record" in your own mind.

# 2. Play Connect the Dots

Years ago I read a quote in which someone who worked for a company that sold educated hunches to businesses explained how he came to some of his conclusions. He said that he combed hundreds of trade and technical journals for early, isolated clues that, when connected, conveyed an "unintended message." I thought that was good advice for anyone marketing products to consumers, but it struck me later that it was also terrific guidance for assessing people on a gut level.

One isolated incident may not tell you anything definitive about someone, but if you're paying attention, you may be able to see a pattern emerge in two or three small incidents. This works especially well for good girls. If your natural inclination is to dismiss a warning sign, playing connect the dots forces you to see a pattern.

I once had a boss who suddenly seemed to be out of the office more than he was in. Whenever I dropped by his office he was at a convention in the Caribbean or a conference in Dallas or whatever. The trips could all have been classified as "junkets" rather than pure taking-care-of-business trips. I saw a little red flag go up, but I dismissed it when I heard him talking about how productive one of the trips had been. Then, a few weeks later, we had a catch-up lunch. As I talked about some of the exciting new opportunities on the horizon, he did something I had never seen him do in a meeting with me: He yawned.

Now, that yawn alone might not have told me anything. It might have simply meant he was overworked—or I was being a bore. But that yawn along with the junkets was an unintended message—this guy had lost interest, had mentally checked out of the organization. And I knew at that moment that I couldn't expect him still to be running the show six months down the road. But as bad as I felt, seeing the handwriting on the wall also allowed me to gather my thoughts and plan for changes. When he left two months later, I didn't have to pick myself up from the floor.

# 3. Use the Gutsy-Girl Pause

One of the best ways to get a read on people is to talk to them, to ask them questions. But you have to be patient. The first thing out of their mouths is often the party line or a lot of patter. You need to wait, say nothing, and hear what they say *next*.

Psychotherapist Marjorie Lapp explains that when you pause, you give someone the opportunity to think over what they've just said and they may begin to elaborate or modify.

# 4. And While You're Pausing, "Watch" What They Say

Sometimes people don't know how to tell you what's going on with them. And so you have to watch them. This is something that Rosalyn Clement, a dynamic property manager for Compass Management and Leasing in Sacramento, trained herself to do. In her field, if you neglect to pick up on any discontent, you may be in for major problems: Your tenant can up and leave. She's learned to be a careful observer. "Sometimes I'll be sitting with a client and someone younger on my staff will be babbling away and I realize that's probably what I used to do. But I now know to watch. If someone is leaning back, arms crossed, eyes glazed over, I know he hasn't told me what's really the matter."

I wrote lots of articles about body language when I was in my twenties, in part because I was so fascinated by it. I wanted to learn what each and every movement meant. What was the message behind a nose twitch? Did crossed arms and legs really mean someone was inaccessible? But what I discovered from one of the researchers I interviewed, Dr. Alan

Mazur of Syracuse University, was that it doesn't have to be that complicated. You can understand it without having to learn a particular "language."

"If you simply pay attention, you'll *know* something is going on," says Mazur. "As human beings we're built to read the body signals of one another." Mazur explains there are really just two areas you need to observe: a person's stress level, which manifests itself in behavior like fidgeting, and a person's affiliative behavior—whether or not he seems to be trying to connect with you with smiles and body "openness."

## 5. Develop Validators for Your Gut Reactions

Houston political consultant Sue Walden, president of Walden and Associates, whose clients have included Sen. Kay Hutchison, says that though a big part of politics is looking at numbers, when it comes to the players in the game, you have to trust your gut. For her, one of the most helpful tools has been networking. "I'm always networking," Walden says, "and when I do I'm a sponge for information. It's when I'm networking that I often pick up the information that validates what my gut has been telling me."

## TRUST YOUR GUT—BUT DON'T ADMIT IT

Unless you're in a fairly high-ranking position, do not say you arrived at a decision because of "intuition" or a "gut feeling." Only the most creative bosses will appreciate such a skill. It's generally better to have people assume you have fantastic resources and a brilliantly analytical mind.

# CHAPTER
# ELEVEN ...................................

# Strategy #9: A Gutsy Girl Takes Smart Risks

If you asked me to describe the biggest risk I've taken in my career, I wouldn't have to think for a second. It was accepting the job of editor-in-chief of *Working Woman* when I was seven and a half months' pregnant.

Why, you might ask, would a woman in her right mind accept a challenging new job when she was less than two months from delivering a baby? Granted, it was wonderful proof that there was at least one enlightened man in the world—the one who hired me. But if you look beyond the small step for the betterment of working women, what you're left with is the fact that there is only so much one woman can do in twenty-four hours. How could I have invited that much stress into my life?

Well, the truth is that when I went on the job interview, I didn't have any serious interest in the position and I *never* assumed I'd be considered for it. I was not only pregnant, but I'd been editing *Child*, a parenting magazine, hardly the foundation for a position as editor-in-chief of a business publication. But several people had recommended me to the owner of *Working Woman* and I'd said yes to the interview just for the opportunity to meet him. He was known for being an entrepreneurial wizard, and I figured he'd be a great contact for later down the road.

Well, as so often happens when there's nothing to lose, I performed terrifically, the way Olympic figure skaters do during the closing night exhibition *after* all the medals have been awarded. I was relaxed, loose, daring. (I also think the pregnancy hormones coursing through my system provided me with extra oomph.) When the owner asked what I would do with *Working Woman*, I found myself totally inspired and energized. I pulled ideas out of the air, I painted a thrilling future for the magazine, and I even jumped to my feet several times to make a point. I did everything, actually, but perform a number from *Cats*. With nothing at stake, I gave a great interview—and much to my shock was offered the job three days later.

The night I accepted the position, I lay in bed ruminating about the risk I was taking. What if I delivered early? What if the baby had a three-month case of colic like my first child had? But over the next few days those risks began to pale in comparison to another one. You see, as I started to take a closer look at the magazine (compared to the perfunctory glance I'd given it before the interview), I realized I didn't "get it" or relate to it on any level. It was filled with dense, specialized articles like "How Leasing Employees Saves Time and Money," "Sweet Success in Sales Automation," and "How to Keep Your Finger on the Pulse of Productivity." The reader obviously spoke some kind of secret language that I had no familiarity with. I began to feel this sickening sense that I had bitten off more than I could chew. How could I generate ideas on subject matter I knew nothing about? It was as if I'd accepted the job as editor of *Astrophysics* magazine, or, worse, had taken a job *as* an astrophysicist. I felt like I was living the nightmare of the actor who finds herself in a play for which she has never learned the lines.

It was my husband who helped me see the light, as I sat there bemoaning my fate several days before I started.

"It's just new-job anxiety," he said.

"No, it isn't," I snapped. "I can't do this job. I know nothing about the subject matter, nothing about the reader."

"How can you say that?" he asked, astonished. "Aren't *you* a working woman?"

I thought a moment and then began to laugh. He was right, of course. I might be in a more "artsy" line of work than the middle managers in the target audience, but nonetheless I supervised people, oversaw a budget, hired and fired. I wasn't nearly the outsider I'd convinced myself I was.

That day I reached a new conclusion about risk: 85 percent of the terror a risk generates depends on the perspective you choose to have.

# WHY GOOD GIRLS HATE RISKY BUSINESS

Taking risks is an essential part of success in business. A survey of 600 professional men and women at large companies by Wick and Company, a management consulting firm, found that 60 percent defined their crucial developmental experiences as "being at risk in a novel or unsupervised environment."

A risk could mean pushing the envelope and attempting something on the cutting edge in your approach to your job. It could also mean taking on a new job that isn't one notch above the one you have, but two or three.

Without risk taking, you can never have any major success. Frank Farley, a psychologist and professor at the University of Wisconsin, who has studied both risk taking and the elements of life success, says the two are completely intertwined. "All my research has pointed to the fact that success equals self-knowledge plus motivation—and self-knowledge comes from risk taking."

Good girls feel uncomfortable with risk taking, but is it any wonder?

From the moment girls are born, their parents may attempt to protect them from the world. According to pyschologist Dr. Allana Elovson, research shows that when baby girls start to crawl, they are more likely than boys to be discouraged from being daring in their explorations.

In school, girls may feel inhibited about risk taking. According to the Sadkers, boys are allowed more exploratory behavior, the kind that teaches you that there is treasure to be found in uncharted territory. Boys, say the Sadkers, are asked to demonstrate in science class three out of four times. They're more likely to be asked questions that call for thought, rather than simply a black or white answer. Teachers also wait longer for them to answer, which encourages them to mentally play with ideas. Many girls grow up encouraged to believe that it's better to be safe than sorry, that getting their dresses dirty is the worst sin in the world.

There may be something else hindering you from making bold moves. A study in the mid-eighties reported that taking risks and possibly failing was stressful for many women because they viewed themselves as operating in a "glass house." If you're the only woman at your level in a company or one of the few in your area, the risks you take—and the failures you experience as an inevitable by-product of some of your risk taking—are going to be far more scrutinized. Your risk taking may be less tolerated or less indulged than that of the guy sitting across the hall.

# THE LITTLE SECRET TO BEING FEARLESS

Now, I'd like to be able to say that I have five pointers that will make you one of the world's gutsiest risk takers starting tomorrow. Unfortunately, that's not the case. According to Dr. Farley, how big a risk taker you are depends to a large degree on your biological makeup. Some people have a genetic factor that enables them—actually compels them—to take big risks, to go way beyond the status quo. He calls them Type T (thrill-seeking) personalities. Its the Type Ts who shape the world because they are the great experimenters, the people who go up the mountain, across the ocean, into the jungle. It's not only nearly impossible to squelch this type of personality, it's also impossible to develop it if you weren't born with the right genes. At the other end of the spectrum are what Dr. Farley calls little ts, people who get nervous just driving to the next town.

Don't get discouraged. Though you can't turn yourself into a major risk taker, if you fall somewhere in the middle ground between Big Ts and little ts, you can improve your comfort level with taking risks and your ability to handle them. Whereas it's hard to squelch a Big T, people in the middle zone can have their risk-taking instincts flattened by the experiences they have in their families and in school. If you stood up and challenged the math theorem, only to be shot down by the teacher, you were probably gun shy the next time you had an adventurous thought. Dr. Farley says, however, that even as an adult, you can find your way back to some of your natural instincts.

The secret is to practice. "When you take a risk, it's very reinforcing," says Farley. "There's a sense of exhilaration, empowerment, that feeling of 'I did it.'" In other words, if you're a good girl who hasn't tried much risk taking, put your toe in the water. Once you get over the jolt and experience the refreshing feel of it, you're going to start thinking about getting your thighs wet, too.

## THE RIGHT WAY TO TAKE A RISK

Of course, that wonderful sense of exhilaration and empowerment won't happen if you take risks and repeatedly land hard on your derrière. That only reinforces your instincts to play it safe. What you need before you take any risk is a four-point plan of protection:

## 1. Give a Risk a Different Name

Even if you commit to going forward on a project that holds plenty of risks, if you remain anxious about it, that anxiety will turn you into an unfortunate expert on late-night infomercials and possibly stifle your decision making at key turning points in the project.

That's why you've got to try to see the experience from a new angle. Dr. Farley stresses that "relabeling" a risk can be an effective way of feeling more in control.

That's essentially what my husband did for me when I went to *Working Woman*. By asking, "Aren't *you* a working woman?" he changed my position: I was no longer "out of my element," but rather a perfectly appropriate choice. From there I also began to see that my ignorance about the world of management could be used as a strength. I could look at the magazine as a brand-new reader would. In fact, there were plenty of readers who were aspirants rather than successful managers, and much of the "managementese" in the magazine was probably foreign to them as well.

And, you know, something interesting began to happen once I changed my perspective. As I looked at the magazine purely as a new reader, much of what in my panic had seemed foreign and impenetrable now struck me as simply dry and dull. I began to think about how much fun it would be to introduce features that were not only informative but also had some sass. I assigned articles like "The Nine Worst Business Books of All Time (Plus the Ten Best)" and "SEX . . . Now That We Have Your Attention, Here's How to Get Everybody Else's."

So come up with a new name for the precipice you are standing on.

- It could be terrifying—or it could be challenging.
- It could be foreign—or it could be intriguing.
- It could expose your ignorance—or your ability to learn.

# 2. Know Exactly What You Have to Lose

Every gutsy girl I've talked to about risk says that one of the first things she does before even thinking about taking a leap is to calculate what's at stake. Is it $30,000 or $300,000? A major client or a minor one? And then how much is that loss going to matter to her department and company's future—and her personal future as well?

Several years ago I had the chance to meet Dr. Pamela Lipkin, a very successful facial plastic surgeon in New York City and one of the few women in the field (no, I haven't done anything yet). Dr. Lipkin says that her approach to assessing risk—and in her field there's plenty of it—boils down to a simple phrase: "Can I live with whatever happens?"

She not only asks herself this question in regard to each procedure she's about to perform, but she also posed it to herself when she had to make a critical choice as she tried to build her practice. The standard way to start a medical practice, she says, is to use family money to buy one or else develop one through the help of the old boy network. Neither approach was available to Lipkin: she had no money, and it was clear that she would never be invited to join the club. So she made her mark by doing something that was taboo in the business. She did revision work—fixes of other doctors' botched jobs—and she *talked* about it.

"When a patient's unhappy with plastic surgery," says Dr. Lipkin, "she may go to other doctors to see if they can help her, but she'll never find anyone who will say, 'This is bad.' It's a boys' club and they won't admit the work wasn't good. Instead, they'll say something like, 'It didn't heal well.' When these patients started to come to me, I offered them something no one else would. I'd say, 'Yeah, I can fix it,' though I would be honest and tell them it wouldn't look as good as it would have if I'd done it originally."

Taking revision cases and talking openly about it was a major risk, one that meant burning her bridges, says Lipkin. "Then there was a magazine article about me called 'The Miracle Worker,' and it was like an invitation to declare war on a small country. It annoyed every doctor in town."

And yet, Lipkin knew that those people weren't ever going to help her anyway. She looked at how much being "the revision doctor" could hurt her—and she knew she could live with it.

# 3. Take Smart Risks Rather Than Stupid Ones

This is where you get to take advantage of that good-girl tendency to do lots and lots of homework. Though you don't want to be one of those oil wildcatters who never gets around to drilling, gathering all the facts is your best form of protection. A gutsy girl never just wings it.

Gail Evans, the dynamic senior VP at CNN/Turner Broadcasting, is the epitome of the smart risk taker. She helped create a central booking operation for CNN to handle the hundreds of guests each week ("from prime ministers to people talking about sex and the single girl") so that different shows wouldn't all be scrambling for the same guests when there was a major news event to cover.

"My ability to take risks," says Evans, "has been greatly enhanced by living every day in front of Ted Turner, someone who has risked the ball game a hundred times and never gotten caught up in worrying about the people who said it couldn't be done. But at the same time, I never do anything by the seat of my pants. I make sure I'm better informed than anyone else. My fail-safe systems are redundant. If the booker wants to put on someone who is an expert on nuclear widgets, the researcher talks to him, too. Everyone is interviewed by two people. When you're trying to be creative, to take risks, you need to cover all your bases, to operate from a solid foundation."

Part of covering your bases is not doing anything without telling the right people. If you take a risk without informing your boss, and it works, the success may be overshadowed by her annoyance at being left out of the loop. If you don't tell people and you fail, you will be all alone in the wilderness, with the lions licking their chops.

# 4. Give Yourself a Safety Net

A risk, by its very definition, is something that could fail. That's why you need, if possible, a safety net, something to break the fall.

There are all kinds of safety nets. There's the cushion you leave in your budget, for instance, to cover your loss. But the nice tight net I see gutsy girls use is their allies. When you have allies, they will support your risks, give you the help you need, and may even assist you in cleaning up any mess. If you sense you are without enough allies, return to Chapter 7.

# HOW TO CONVINCE YOUR BOSS OR CLIENT TO GO ALONG

No matter how good a job you've done convincing yourself that a risk is worth taking, unless you're the head of your company, you're now going to have to convince someone else of the same thing. Of course, a major part of convincing your boss or upper management or a client to go along with your plan is to brief them as thoroughly as possible and be able to answer any questions. But that's not enough. Though management consultants stress these days that American business is in dire need of smart risk taking, many senior managers are scaredy cats. They are likely to balk at plans that will cost money, violate the usual way of doing things, and possibly make them look reckless. You may have to try some fancy stuff to get them to go along.

I think I'm pretty good at convincing bosses to take risky leaps, though it's something I've learned by trial and error. I remember being twenty-five and trying to convince Ruth Whitney, the editor-in-chief of *Glamour*, to let me go with a team of scientists on a sonar search for the Loch Ness monster and write about my experiences. Now, the primary reason I wanted the assignment was so that I'd be on a boat with lots of hopefully single male scientists, but I was pitching the idea as if it would totally tantalize the *Glamour* reader. Ruth looked completely skeptical, and asked how I could make the piece newsy with *Glamour*'s three-month lead time. "What if I sleep with the Loch Ness monster?" I replied. Needless to say, I wasn't in Scotland before ye.

It goes without saying that no one is going to back a risk of yours unless they think there's something in it for them. I'm pretty sure I knew that at twenty-five, but I thought I could get around an idea's obvious lack of merit with a little charm and a lot of BS. I'd never try that today because I know I'd pay for it down the road.

Let's say your idea is one that makes absolute sense for your boss to get behind. That's still no guarantee that she'll say yes. I've come to see that there are three things, *beyond* having a strong idea and the research to back it up, that can help convince the skeptical.

The first is to anticipate their objections and present them as your own. Sure you could wait for them to raise them and then sound brilliantly prepared as you counter, but that creates a you-versus-them situation. Don't let it get to that. Say something like "Now, of course, a major concern with this approach would be X, but as I investigated, I learned that it wasn't really a problem."

The next is to whip out the visual aids. When I went to management consultant Judy Markus to learn how to give better presentations, she told me that her philosophy is to use visual tools any time you possibly can, even when you're pitching a small idea to your boss rather than giving a major presentation. The first time I tried this strategy with my boss I felt kind of silly, as if I'd asked him at lunch if he needed me to cut up his meat for him.

But I soon saw how effective it was. Most people, no matter how smart, aren't capable of hearing your idea and then mentally conjuring up how fabulous it will be. The more you can help them along with visuals, the better. I don't mean lots of tedious black-and-white overheads, but rather nifty, colorful charts and pictures.

The third thing you've got to do is seem fiercely passionate—and unfortunately, that can be hard to do when you're nervous. I've found that fear tends to sit on the part of the brain that produces enthusiasm, resulting in a monotone delivery and no spark.

Just last year, I learned a fabulous new trick for letting your passion through. An ad agency was making a presentation to us at *McCall's* on a possible campaign to solicit subscribers. Several people at the agency gave background information and then the senior copywriter, Karen Mischke, stood up to present the actual idea. The concept was strong, but what really helped hook us was her delivery. It was so good, in fact, that I called her later and asked her what her secret was.

She said that someone once had taught her that when presenting an idea you should always try to share with the listener the "process" you'd been through in developing the idea. It not only relaxes you to do so, because it's like telling a story, but it also adds credibility—you've obviously done your research and considered all the angles.

In Mischke's case, she started off telling us that she was in many ways exactly like the women who would be getting the direct-mail campaign for *McCall's*. Her mother had read *McCall's* and she had assumed it was a magazine for older women. When she opened it she was surprised to discover that it was geared for women in their thirties and forties. She talked about the articles she liked and how she would use the advice in her own life.

Mischke laughingly told me that sharing the process was really what Melanie Griffith had done in one of the classic scenes in *Working Girl*. "Remember," she said, "when Melanie's character, Tess, gets found out, but the head guy of Trask Industry gives her the chance to prove that the great idea was hers, not Sigourney Weaver's? Tess explains how she clipped a story from *Fortune* on how Trask was considering branching into broadcasting and then she saw the gossip columnist's story on the radio deejay and so she starts putting these ideas together in her mind until she thinks, What about Trask getting into radio? The guy is mesmerized listening to her and then thoroughly convinced. She took him through her thinking process and that made all the difference."

# HOW TO STAY COOL UNDER PRESSURE

You've set everything in motion and now you must wait for the results. Terrifying, isn't it?

When a good girl finally takes a risk, she is likely to project about the future, imagining the absolute worst that could happen. She might tell herself she's preparing for all possible outcomes and therefore it's a healthy exercise—but it's not.

Sandy Hill Pittman, an adventurer and mountaineer whose personal goal is to climb the highest mountain on every continent (only the Mount Everest summit has eluded her due to weather conditions), says that one of the most disruptive and dangerous things you can do on a risky climb is to let the mind "meander." On her last Everest climb she practiced what she calls "walking meditation," focusing on one step at a time. "Without thinking," she says, "I walked lighter, stumbled less, and found my center." This same technique will work for you with any kind of business risk.

# WHAT TO DO WHEN YOU FEEL IN OVER YOUR HEAD

Sometimes, no matter how prepared you are for a risk, you can end up feeling as if you've ended up with more than you bargained for. This is most likely to happen in a brand-new job. You're experienced, you're skilled, you're game, but the challenge is just, well, bigger and harder than you ever anticipated.

When a good girl finds herself in this kind of situation, she starts thinking in very drastic terms, like I'm in over my head, or, I've bitten off more than I can chew. Men, on the other hand, don't think of drowning or choking. Rather they view a tough new job as a *stretch*. Right now it's out of their grasp, but if they just reach a little farther, try a little harder, it soon can be theirs. Perhaps this way of thinking comes from years of listening to beer commercials stressing that you must grab for all the gusto you can get.

The fastest way to get over the sinking-fast feeling is to accelerate your learning curve. Critical information will not only help you make smart decisions and cope with what is coming your way, but the activity of information gathering has a way of distracting you from any terror at hand. However, that said, you don't want to look like you're scrambling. A couple of my favorite techniques for information gathering that don't make you look desperate: Ask questions of people as if you were soliciting their opinion rather than feeling needy for help. ("What do *you* think are the most critical issues facing the department right now?") or ask them to do the information gathering for you as part of a special project.

When I got to *Working Woman*, I had plenty to learn, but I certainly wasn't going to reveal my ignorance by asking questions like "Could someone please tell me what the hell the phrase 'pancake management' means?" What I did was have editors hand in special reports for me on a variety of topics. For instance, I asked for a list and critique of the best career writers in the country, theoretically so I could pick one as a columnist, but it also served as a manual for me, taking me up to speed on everything of importance being said on the subject.

# HOW TO KEEP THE WOLVES AT BAY

No matter how much self-assurance you've demonstrated in a risky situation, particularly a new job, you may look up one day to see the wolves circling. I think that when you're in a new position it's best to do as much one-on-one work as possible and avoid group settings. People are less receptive and enthusiastic in a pack situation, because they're watching everyone else. They also can get mean.

The first time I had a job that involved managing seven or eight people, the woman I was replacing, who had accepted a new position at the magazine, kept recommending to me that I organize a "Get-to-know-Kate" breakfast for everybody who would be reporting to me. Absolutely nothing about the idea appealed to me, and yet I knew that I was going to annoy this woman if I didn't do as she suggested.

It still makes me cringe to think of that morning. There I sat next to a coffee urn the size of a silo and a platter of blueberry muffins, with seven women who looked like they would rather be anywhere else, even the International House of Pancakes, than sitting in a circle with me. No matter how *inclusive* I was trying to be in my talk, there was a them-versus-me feeling. Besides, I wasn't sounding very smart. I would have been much more effective and demonstrated far more clout if

I'd met with people one at a time, to talk to them about my plans and ask them about their own needs and opinions.

# THE ONE PHRASE YOU SHOULD NEVER UTTER EVEN IF YOU FEEL IT:

"I'm not sure."

# THE GUTSY GIRL'S GUIDE TO TAKING THE HEAT

When a good girl takes a risk that fails, her inclination is to assume all the blame, and wear a hair shirt for an indefinite period of time. Or, perhaps even worse, to hibernate in her office, hoping everything will blow over if she wishes hard enough. Though these approaches may make you feel better or safer, they are both extremely dangerous: They can create the impression that the situation—and your culpability—are far worse than they are.

Some of what I've learned about taking the heat has come from my friend Merrie Spaeth, president of Spaeth Communications, who specializes in helping companies talk to the public when they have a major crisis on their hands. There was a time when some companies in crisis would close ranks and keep their mouths shut, only making matters worse. Spaeth will coach an organization on how to tell the story so that management comes across as honest, responsible, and proactive.

Though coping with a bank failure is not exactly the same as dealing with a setback in your work, several of the same principles apply. You have to be gutsy enough to make a full disclosure and you also have to manage the communication effectively.

First, says Spaeth, put everything in writing. That's your protection against any rewriting of history a boss or co-worker might attempt down the road. It's also the opportunity to remind everybody of how many players endorsed the plan—also known as spreading the blame. It's not that you're trying to shirk responsibility. But if you were headed in a direction that management encouraged and your game plan was given an enthusiastic go-ahead, you don't want to be holding all the blame. And believe me, people will try to make that happen. Use words like *we, our,* and *together*.

There are two other things you want to keep in mind when you're putting together your written documentation. Use as many positive words as possible, steering away from the negative ones. You also should offer a solution or damage control. "If the new branch in the northwest mall didn't work out," says Spaeth, "offer a great plan for dealing with the inventory from there."

In addition to putting things in writing, you should talk to as many of the key players as you can in person. Spaeth says that it's a way to make sure they're informed, but also to get a glimmer if anyone is trying to bad-mouth you over what's happened.

# CHAPTER
## TWELVE ..................................

# A GUTSY GIRL'S GUIDE TO THE FUTURE

Up until now, all the gutsy-girl strategies I've talked about relate to the job you have at this moment in time. But if you want long-term career success, it's not enough to be gutsy in your day-to-day work. You must also take a gutsy approach to plotting your career, aggressively using both your expertise and your contacts to get you better and better positions up the ladder.

Even if you currently love your job and you're a blazing success at it, you must be looking toward the future. A gutsy girl never rests on her laurels or allows herself to get too comfy in a job. In the Korn Ferry study of executive women, 80 percent of the participants said they believe that strategic job changes are an important element in achieving success.

A gutsy girl, therefore, is always scouting, making contacts, and researching opportunities in her field—as well as other fields that pique her interest. It's quite likely that you could have two, perhaps even three careers in your lifetime.

A gutsy girl also knows that the best time to get a great new job is, surprisingly, not when she's discontent with her current position but when she's absolutely in love with it. That way she's operating from a position of strength, able to capitalize on both her reputation as a passionate worker and also her full-blown self-confidence. She realizes, as well, that sometimes she must grab hold of an opportunity even when she doesn't feel 100 percent ready to handle it.

Sounds scary, doesn't it? But all you have to do is take the nine strategies a gutsy girl uses in her job and apply them to growing your career *beyond* that job.

# 1. A Gutsy Girl Breaks the Rules

There seem to be hundreds of rules in existence about careers. If you want to get hired by a tony law firm, you have to have attended an Ivy League school. If you want to make it as a television reporter, you have to start at a small station "out of town." If you want to work for such-and-such company, you should send your résumé directly to the human resources department.

Most of these rules exist for a reason. They reflect reality, the experiences countless people have had. But each rule is based on the odds. It may have been true for *most* people—but certainly not all of them. What a gutsy girl knows is that many of these rules will limit her if she chooses to follow them. To make as much headway as possible, she must break the rules or at least go around them.

The first thing you must do is question every rule you hear about the field you're in and what it takes to be a success in it. When I think back on my early career, I realize that I automatically bought into so many of them, as if I'd been brainwashed by the career control squad. I've come to believe that some of the rules actually are perpetuated because people in certain industries are extremely greedy and like to make their fields appear impenetrable. When I was thinking of making a career shift to the television industry in my twenties, I attended several seminars on the TV business, and every thirty-year-old producer began his or her presentation with this rule: "The TV business is almost *impossible* to break into." It was as if they wanted to discourage anyone else from competing with them for the best jobs.

Though I took for granted many of the rules I heard, I soon spotted a few gutsy women who didn't. One of these women joined the articles department when I was at *Glamour* and had a profound effect on my thinking.

First, a little background on the rules of publishing. The main one I heard when I visited the personnel departments of magazine companies when I was twenty-two was that to break in you "absolutely have to start as a secretary slash editorial assistant." I balked at the idea, but acquiesced when I saw that I wasn't going to get in the door without going that route.

Within several years I'd been promoted to a feature writer, working with a bunch of other young editors and writers who had paid their dues the way I had. One day we heard that a new writer was joining the staff. And you know what? She was fresh out of college. She was also the author of an article that would soon appear in the magazine.

She and I became fast friends and the first thing I wanted to know from Amy was how she'd pulled it off. It turned out that through a contact at journalism class, she had landed an interview with the managing editor rather than having to go through the personnel department, as everyone else had (Broken Rule Number One). Then, when the managing editor gave her the start-as-a-secretary spiel, she asked how someone got hired as a writer rather than a secretary. The editor explained that you had to have *written* something. Amy went home and wrote a charming article on how to survive living with your parents when you're just out of college and looking for a job. It had a youthful irreverence that made it different from traditional *Glamour* articles. I still remember this funny line about how she'd spend Saturday nights reading and picking at her pimples while her parents entertained downstairs (Broken Rule Number Two). They accepted the article and gave her a job as a writer rather than a secretary (Broken Rule Number Three).

Listening to her saga, my first thought was how naive I'd been never to challenge the conventional wisdom. My second thought was that I'd never do it again.

Once you've heard a rule and questioned it, ask yourself what are the possible ways to get around it. Be creative, be adventurous, be daring.

# 2. A Gutsy Girl Has One Clear Goal for the Future

One of the mistakes that's easy to make as a good girl is to expend so much energy doing your job that you never take time to think beyond it and plot a brilliant career for yourself. You may even assume that your company has a plan for you, one that you should allow to unfold. Be flattered if your boss says she has big things in mind for you, but never, ever sit around waiting for them to happen.

A gutsy girl has a gutsy career plan. She not only actively looks outside her present job for ways to facilitate that mission, but she also makes certain choices in her job to make sure the plan becomes a reality. She'll take advantage of opportunities to develop an expertise or specialty, raise her technology IQ, learn a foreign language, improve her public speaking, and refine her leadership skills.

That's not to say you should have a *rigid* plan. Remember a few years ago when we were all supposed to have a response ready when an interviewer asked us, "Where do you see yourself in five years"? Maybe there are still a few moronic interviewers who would expect you to have an answer to that question, but you shouldn't have to know—nor should you want to.

I think what you need instead are a variety of possibilities—one of which is eventually having your *own* business. Think in broad strokes, but stay focused. Remember the trick of using three or four words to sum up your plan? That's what my friend Merrie Spaeth has done in plotting her career. At fourteen she starred with Peter Sellers in *The World of Henry Orient*. She's been a newspaper columnist, TV host, magazine writer, businesswoman, political candidate, assistant to the head of the FBI, media adviser to President Reagan, and now she's the head of her own communications company (and that's only a partial list). At twenty-nine there's no way she could have told anyone what she would be doing in five years. But there are three terms, she says, that she considers as mission words for herself: "leadership, power, and high profitability."

# 3. A Gutsy Girl Does Only What's Essential

Whenever a good-girl friend of mine is on a job quest and I ask her how she's doing, the reply I seem to get most often is, "I'm still working on my résumé."

Just as a good girl gets into the good-girl spin on the job, working harder than she has to and refusing to take shortcuts, so she approaches her job hunt. She spends weeks putting together the "perfect" résumé, sends it to the "right" people, and dutifully waits to hear.

A gutsy girl knows, however, that she must cut through all the tape. Forget doing mounds of research on the organizational chart, trying to find out whom you should be talking to. Pick up the phone, call your friend whose cousin works there, and ask *her*. Forget composing a "perfect" résumé. Write a gutsy cover letter that tells exactly why you'd love to work at that company. Forget the human resources department. Go directly to the source.

A gutsy girl also knows that one of the best shortcuts is to do two things simultaneously. Whereas a good girl wrestles with the question, "Should I look for a new job or should I try to get more responsibility in this one?" a gutsy girl pursues both courses of action simultaneously and takes the first prize she gets.

# 4. A Gutsy Girl Doesn't Worry Whether People Like Her

A good girl's pleaser instincts can get in her way during her job hunt, just as they can in her work. You may be reluctant to pursue a new position because you don't want to leave your boss in the lurch during the budget process—or just after you've been given a nice new title and raise. You may feel guilty about leaving the people in your department, especially if you've hired them away from other companies. You may worry that people will be "mad" at you if you jump ship.

They probably will be mad, but they'll get over it.

Though there are certain circumstances in which you can't be worried about what people think, you must nonetheless be constantly building a network of people who will help you in your career pursuits. Stay in touch with former bosses and friendly colleagues. Do favors where possible. Ask for favors when you need them. Write lots of thank-you notes. Since

*Glamour*, every job I've gotten has been a result of someone I know giving my name to the person who was looking.

# 5. A Gutsy Girl Walks and Talks Like a Winner

If you've always felt uncomfortable strutting your stuff in your job, you'll probably feel even more squeamish at the thought of doing it *outside* your company. In the thick of my good-girl days, I hesitated to toot my own horn on job interviews not only because it felt as foreign to me as playing the bagpipes, but also because I believed that it would be downright offensive. In the back of my mind I had this idea that modesty would actually work to my advantage. I'd speak of my accomplishments in a reserved manner and tell myself that once the interviewer heard via the grapevine or from my references that I was stronger than I'd indicated, I'd get extra points for not being a braggart.

I changed my entire viewpoint when, years ago, I interviewed a man for a position on my staff. This guy came into my office in an Armani suit and tie and spent forty-five minutes telling me what a fabulous job he'd done at the last place he'd worked (the other fifteen minutes he used to tell me what a fabulous job *I'd* done during my career). He made his current position sound as if it carried as much clout as Secretary of State. He'd recruited this writer and that writer and had brilliantly edited their copy. He even used certain words to describe himself, like *rainmaker*.

As he displayed his feathers like the yellow-breasted bower bird, part of me was thinking, God, this guy is too slick for words. But you know what? Another part of me was thinking how fabulous it would be to have somebody on the staff with this much gumption and passion and panache.

Take everything you've learned about walking and talking like a winner in your job and apply it to your job hunt.

# 6. A Gutsy Girl Asks for What She Wants

Asking for what you want is tough no matter where you do it, but at least when you ask in your current job you know the lay of the land and you have a sense of how much someone has to give and how likely they are to give it. When you're up for a new job, you're working in almost total darkness. There are a couple of principles that should guide you:

- Always, always ask for more. Good girls fear that if they push too hard, they'll end up losing everything. The key is to ask for more while sounding totally enthusiastic about the job and making a deal happen. Tell them, "I'm thrilled you're offering me the position and I'm very, very interested. However, I'm looking for X amount and I hope there's a way to make that happen."
- Ask now because you won't have nearly as much leverage later. What a good girl tells herself—as an excuse not to be too assertive—is, I can always get more once I get there. Well, once they have you, they are far, far less generous. Go for everything now.
- Ask for what isn't there. In her job, a gutsy girl knows that just because no one else has it doesn't mean she can't get it. The same principle applies in your job campaign. After my boss left *Family Weekly* and I'd lost the editor-in-chief position to an outsider, I knew it was time to get my act in gear and go elsewhere. The new editor seemed happy with me and I didn't feel in any immedi-

ate danger, but it was time to capitalize on my position while I still could.

The ink on my résumé was barely dry (this was before the personal computer) when the editor-in-chief of *Mademoiselle*, whom I had written freelance articles for when she was at *Ladies' Home Journal*, asked me to join the magazine as articles editor. It was a terrific position, with the opportunity to work with fabulous writers, and yet it didn't seem like the right next step for me. I turned down the job and she asked me to think about it some more. Finally I realized what was bothering me: the *title*. Even though *Family Weekly* didn't have the same stature as *Mademoiselle*, I would be going from a title of executive editor to a less prestigious one. I went for broke and said I would accept the job if the title was changed to executive editor. Though there was already an executive editor, they made me one, too.

# 7. A Gutsy Girl Faces Trouble Head-On

As I said in Chapter 9, it took me a long time to realize that everyone at work is a *potential* sabatoeur. It took me even longer to realize that the same holds true when you're going after a position in a new area or company.

You are far less likely to suspect these saboteurs because you hardly know them. Often, they end up sandbagging you not because they have anything against you personally, but because they are simply unreliable or ignorant—or maybe they're just busybodies. Some of these hidden-saboteur situations may be:

- The human resources person whom you've talked to

about wanting to explore options in another department tells your boss what you're up to.

- Someone at the outside company you're applying to mentions to several people in the industry that you're interviewing there.
- One of the references you've given offers a mediocre evaluation of you.
- A headhunter who doesn't appreciate your value blocks you from becoming a candidate.
- An acquaintance at the company you're interviewing with hurts your candidacy with "inside" information. (i.e., "She's thinking of starting a family.")
- After you leave a company, people at your old job rewrite history and paint you as weak in several areas, and their remarks work their way back to your new boss.

What can you do about these kinds of sabotage? Because they're likely to happen out of your range of view, your best course of action is prevention:

- Tell as few people as possible about your plans—and never tell a peer who might consider herself a rival.
- Never call someone and simply warn her that you're using her as a reference. Ask if she feels comfortable with the idea. If she seems at all hesitant, don't use her.
- Keep in mind that though there are many discreet people in human resources, anything you say *could* be used against you.

# 8. A Gutsy Girl Trusts Her Instincts

A golden gut is an essential tool when you're making a career move. With such an overload of factors influencing your decision, you need something to act as your compass. And yet if you're a good girl, you can count on the fact that your gut will experience interference from the usual circuit jammers: a need for consensus, worrying over what other people will think, a reluctance to see the negative.

You need to do your homework and then *feel* your way. When I was offered the job as senior editor of *Family Weekly*, I had a strong inkling that though the magazine was just a newspaper supplement, two notches up from those freestanding inserts with coupons for Tide and double fudge brownies, it would be terrific experience for me. I'd be editing stories on politics, national affairs, and celebrities, an experience I'd never had at *Glamour*. And yet when I told several people about the job offer, they looked horrified. "Why would you want to work *there*?" they asked. I started worrying that once I got there, it would be impossible to use it as a stepping-stone to a position at a classy magazine.

So I did some homework. What I learned when checking around about *Family Weekly* was that someone who'd held the position I was being offered had gone on to a terrific job at another magazine. That was at least one indicator that I wouldn't be trapped in Sunday supplement hell. When you're researching, take heed of anything you find yourself rationalizing or dismissing—for instance, the interviewer is a little fuzzy about how you fit into the chain of command, and you hear yourself mentally saying, I'm sure it'll get sorted out once I get there.

Then let your gut take over. When I met the editor-in-chief of *Family Weekly*, I found him to be extraordinarily smart and charismatic, and I had this sense that not only would it be great fun to work for him, but that his classiness would compensate for any that the magazine lacked. And it did.

And one more thing. Just as people have body language that's essential to watch, so do companies. Frazzled secretaries, sourpusses, an ambience that doesn't reflect a consistent mission are all signs of what's really going on.

# 9. A Gutsy Girl Takes Smart Risks

Just leaving the safe haven of your current job for a new position out there in the big bad world can seem like a major risk, and that can convince you that you've fulfilled your risk quota. New job, new company, new staff, new boss—that's plenty to contend with. But you have to be willing to live more dangerously than that if you want to get the maximum out of changing jobs.

First of all, I think that wherever possible you should try to do a double career jump. What's the next logical position on the ladder for you? Instead of automatically trying to go after that one, consider the rung *above* it. Remember how men learn to think of a risky new situation as a stretch rather than being in over their heads? You need to have the same mindset. Of course, you certainly don't want to mislead anyone about your abilities. But you may be able to end up with a fancier title and more responsibility by going to a smaller company rather than a larger one, a newer one rather than a more established, conservative one.

You also have to be willing to gamble as you pursue a potential position. The first writing job I had at *Glamour* was as a promotion copywriter, which was not really the kind of writing I wanted to do—my dream was to write features for the magazine. In an attempt to get noticed, I started writing short pieces for one of the front-of-the-book editors (my first was a groundbreaking item called "Bridesmaids Dresses You Really *Can* Wear Again"). One day the managing editor asked me if I wanted to take on a more substantial assignment, one they couldn't picture giving to any of the normal people in the features department: She wanted me to spend a day as a guest clown with Ringling Brothers Circus and write about my experience.

Why me? Because she said I was a ham. What she didn't realize was that I was very shy and the idea of performing at Madison Square Garden held as much appeal for me as riding down Second Avenue naked on a skateboard. But I did it, hoping it would be my ticket out of promotion writing. I put on a silly outfit and made little kids cry in the bleachers and did a dopey routine with bad timing, trying not to step in any elephant dung—all the while feeling excruciatingly self-conscious. But you know what? After I handed in the piece, the editor-in-chief offered me a job in the articles department.

Whether you're pursuing a new job or being courted for one, you need to always ask yourself if you're going as far as you should to get their attention, stand out from the pack, leave them with the impression that they can't live without you.

One of my favorite stories: When Pulitzer Prize–winning columnist Anna Quindlen wanted to get hired out of college by the *New York Post*, she followed up her interview with a note in "kidnapped"-style lettering that said, HIRE ANNA QUINDLEN OR YOU SWIM WITH THE FISHES.

## HOW TO ALWAYS BE A GUTSY GIRL

I wish I could end this book by announcing, "Once a gutsy girl, always a gutsy girl." But that isn't necessarily the case. If you've lived your life as a gutsy girl, it's not likely that anything will change you, but if you are a *new* gutsy girl, in other words a reformed good girl, it's more than likely that you'll find your good-girl instincts taking over from time to time. It reminds me of those tiny sponges shaped as dinosaurs that increase ten times their size the minute you toss them into water. There are certain conditions and settings that simply activate your need to please, to play it safe, to shrink from the limelight, to buff a project to death. It may be when you're under stress or when you're in a brand-new work environment or when the psychodynamics of your work setting make you unnecessarily begin to doubt yourself.

That's why as a new gutsy girl you must be vigilant, making certain that you don't fall back into good-girl behavior. Here's what I've found is helpful for me.

# Ask Yourself at the End of Each Day, "Did I Do Anything to Break the Law Today?"

Even once you discover the rewards of rule breaking, it's easy to get out of the habit of doing it. In most work environments you find yourself lured into a routine of taking care of business and maintaining the status quo. It's important to reflect on your behavior regularly and be sure you haven't slipped back into being a Goody Two-Shoes.

One great way to stay active as a renegade is to allow yourself to be inspired by other people's rule breaking—it certainly beats being green with envy. I learned a profound lesson in this during my late twenties, just after I left *Glamour* magazine to seek my fortune elsewhere.

My years at *Glamour* had been terrific, but I had gotten off to a bumpy start. When I went to my first interview with Personnel, I was too embarrassed to admit that I wanted to be a writer (Good Girl Syndrome in overdrive). I mentioned that I'd just spent four months working as a coordinator in an election, and I was swiftly placed as an editorial assistant in the merchandising department. My main responsibility was assisting the merchandising editors in putting on fashion shows in the *Glamour* showroom, which meant that I arranged the chairs, set up the cookies and coffee, and washed—yes washed—the dishes afterwards. I was miserable beyond belief. One day the promotion director of *Glamour*, who worked several offices away, pulled me aside in the hallway. She was about sixty and very eccentric: She wore mostly fake-fur vests and wide pants, carried a cigarette holder, and often called out instructions to her staff as they trailed behind her like poodles. She had never said more than two words to me, so I assumed she was about to complain that I brewed the coffee too strong or wasn't putting out enough petite madeleines on the platter. But instead she said, "I hear you want to be a writer. Why don't you come and work for me? I can't believe we have a *Glamour* college winner washing dishes."

Her name was Katie Gravett, and not only did she save my dishpan hands, but she was a fabulous boss who inspired me every step of the way. There was an aura about her that seemed left over from another era of magazine publishing. She'd known Condé Nast, the great publisher of *Vanity Fair* magazine, and there were photographs in her office of her at El Morocco, with the telltale zebra-print banquettes in the background. Though her basic responsibilities were simply to put on special events and create selling brochures for the advertising salespeople, she ran her department as if she was an empress and everyone treated her that way.

I worked for about six months as her assistant and then she made me one of her promotion copywriters. But she knew what I really wanted to do was write for the magazine and she was thrilled when I finally got offered a position in the feature department. We had lunch regularly, growing to be friends. When I decided, after six years, to leave *Glamour*, she was one of the first people I told.

A short time after I got settled at my new job, Katie and I had lunch at a fancy midtown Chinese restaurant, and to my astonishment she told me she was retiring from *Glamour* and moving with her husband to Rockport, Massachusetts, where she had discovered a wonderful house she hoped to buy. Granted, she was entitled to retire, but I, and everyone else, just assumed she'd be at *Glamour* until the absolute last moment. And then she said the thing that had such a profound effect on me. She told me that she had decided to leave *Glamour* partly because *I* had left. My departure had come as a surprise to her, she said, and it had inspired her to reflect on her own life and recognize that it was time for change. When she opened her fortune cookie at the end of the meal, it said, YOU WILL SOON LIVE IN A NEW HOME.

It was a little scary for me to consider that at twenty-eight I'd had such a major influence on someone's life choice, but since then I have used the lesson Katie taught me on many occasions. Rather than allowing other people's triumphs and turning points to make you envious or depressed, use them as a call to action.

## Think About What You've Been Saying

A lot of good-girl behavior is manifested in the way you speak or *don't* speak. If you've been talking a lot lately, it may be a sign that you're gushing, trying to please. If you've been talking very little, you may not be generating rule-breaking ideas, demonstrating your expertise, tooting your own horn, or asking for what you want.

## Look at Things Through a Guy's Eyes

Though, as I've said over and over, I don't believe you should act like a man, some men are nonetheless extraordinarily gutsy and you should turn to them for their input. More than a few of the gutsy girls I know have told me that they often use men friends and mentors for guidance on all sorts of matters, including rehearsing dialogue for an important interview or confrontation. A friend of mine revealed to me lately that she gives all her important memos to a male friend to review before sending them and he invariably cuts out her first paragraph. "He's made me see that I have a tendency to present lots of unnecessary information when what I really should be doing is cutting to the chase," she says.

When I suspect I'm ready to act like a good girl, I consult with my husband or my brother Jim, who is an investment banker in New York, and they steer me right.

## Spend Some Time with a Little Gutsy Girl

When I started this book, I became hypersensitive about the way I treated my five-year-old daughter, Hayley, and on more than one occasion, I caught myself telling her, "Oh, that's a good girl." I began "watching" the way I dealt with her and tried not to make statements that would reinforce the idea that she had to be the perfect little girl. I got so focused on *my* behavior toward her that it took me a while to realize that this gutsy little girl had a lot to teach me.

Though Hayley has already been exposed in the world to plenty of messages that indicate that boys are entitled to more than girls are, she hasn't yet taken them to heart. She's full of energy and courage and confidence.

One day she was standing next to me as I was looking through my then six-year-old son's closet. She pointed to a Batman rain slicker he used to wear. "Mom," she said, "that slicker is too small for Hunter, isn't it?"

"Yeah, you're right. We should send it to Jeffrey," I answered, referring to my nephew.

"Well, could *I* have it?" she asked.

Needless to say, I felt ashamed. There I was, fueling all the terrible stereotypes of boys as superheros, and girls as sideliners. But after I got done silently berating myself, I allowed myself to be inspired by Hayley.

She wore the slicker to school the next day, with a dress underneath. It was such a cool, hip look, and it was clear she didn't give a darn what anyone thought about her.

She's such an inspiration when I find the good girl taking over. She follows her instincts, loves taking risks, and always asks for what she wants.

And though I know my publisher wouldn't like this, I hope this book is totally obsolete by the time my daughter launches her career.